Date Due

971.102   McMicking, Thomas.
McMi   Overland from Canada to British Columbia /
          by Thomas McMicking ; edited by Joanne Leduc ;
          with illustrations by William G.R. Hind.
          Vancouver : University of British Columbia
          Press, c1981.
              xl, 121 p. : ill., maps. (Recollections
          of the pioneers of British Columbia ; v. 4)
              First published in installments in the
          British Columbian, 1862-1863.
                      (Continued on next card)
          0774801360   142176X   NLC

          6/ex

Overland from Canada

Recollections of the Pioneers of British Columbia

Overland from Canada is the fourth volume in a series of editions of important documents of the colonial and early provincial history of British Columbia.

The first volume is *The Reminiscences of Doctor John Sebastian Helmcken*, edited by Dorothy Blakey Smith. J.S. Helmcken was British Columbia's pioneer doctor, first Speaker in the legislature, and one of the negotiators of the colony's entry into Confederation.

The second volume is *A Pioneer Gentlewoman in British Columbia*, edited by Margaret A. Ormsby. The author of these recollections, Susan Allison, settled in the Similkameen Valley in the 1860's.

The third volume is *God's Galloping Girl*, edited by W.L. Morton. Monica Storrs's diaries describe her mission work on the Peace River frontier during the Depression.

Overland from Canada to British Columbia

By Mr. Thomas McMicking
of Queenston, Canada West

Edited by Joanne Leduc

With illustrations by William G.R. Hind

UNIVERSITY OF BRITISH COLUMBIA PRESS

VANCOUVER AND LONDON

Overland from Canada to British Columbia
By Mr. Thomas McMicking of Queenston, Canada West

©The University of British Columbia 1981

Canadian Cataloguing in Publication Data

McMicking, Thomas.
    Overland from Canada to British Columbia

    First published in installments in the British
Columbian, 1862-1863.
    Bibliography: p.
    Includes index.
    ISBN 0-7748-0136-0

    1. Overland journeys to the Pacific. 2. British
Columbia—History—1849-1871.* 3. Canada—
Description and travel—1760-1867.* I. Leduc,
Joanne, 1943-   II. The British Columbian.
III. Title.
FC3822.M22   971.102   C81-091191-4
F1088. M22

International Standard Book Number 0-7748-0136-0
Printed in Canada

This book has been published with the help of a gift to scholarly publishing made in honour of Dr. Harold S. Foley for his distinguished services to the University of British Columbia,

a grant from The Leon and Thea Koerner Foundation,

a grant from the Canadian Federation for the Humanities, using funds provided by the Social Sciences and Humanities Research Council of Canada,

and it has been financially assisted by the Government of British Columbia through the British Columbia Cultural Fund and the British Columbia Lottery Fund.

CONTENTS

ILLUSTRATIONS

CREDITS

The sketches which appear throughout the text are all from a sketch-book of W.G.R. Hind now in the Public Archives of Canada. The following are the reference numbers given in the sequence in which they appear. C28248, C33719, C33710, C33835, C33757, C33762, C22710, C33837, C28259, C33743, C33722, C33753, C33708, C33704, C33714, C33840, C33759, C33756, C33838, C33761, C33752.

ACKNOWLEDGEMENTS

My first, most important acknowledgement is to Val Sawadsky, who supported me in every way while I worked on this book; and my second is to Victor Hopwood, who drew my attention and that of others to the possibilities of Thomas McMicking's narrative. Dr. Hopwood's own work and our discussions about Overlander material and early Canadian exploration literature have been my inspiration from the beginning. The President's Fund provided an initial research grant.

Dr. Michael Batts of the University of British Columbia and Wilfred Chapple of the Alcuin Society worked hard and participated actively in the early editing of the text. They were instrumental in getting the project off the ground. Anne Yandle of the Special Collections Division, University of British Columbia Library, also took an active interest and has been accommodating and encouraging throughout.

People across Canada, and some in the United States, have responded with generosity to my requests for help. Working westward from Ontario, I wish to thank Richard Landon of the Thomas Fisher Rare Book Library at the University of Toronto, a friend and an ex-British Columbian who retains an interest in the history of his native province; J. Russell Harper, a friend of my late father whose work on W.G.R. Hind has been of much value to this project; also Paul Cornell, Department of History, Waterloo University; Hugh MacMillan, Kenneth Macpherson, and R. Tapscott of the Archives of Ontario; Linda Potter, Niagara-on-the-Lake Public Library; Deborah Rose, Niagara Historical Society; Inge Jahnke Saczkowski, Niagara Falls Public Library; Sheila Wilson, St. Catharines Public Library; and Sheila Moir, Presbyterian Church Committee on History.

In Wisconsin, thanks are due to James L. Hansen and Myrna Williamson of the State Historical Society, and Edwin L. Hill of the Murphy Library, University of Wisconsin at Lacrosse. In Minnesota, Bonnie Wilson and Louis M. De Gryse of the Minnesota Historical Society were very helpful.

In Manitoba, three generous people went out of their way to provide valuable information: Shirlee Anne Smith, Hudson's Bay Company archivist; E. Leigh Syms, staff archaeologist, Brandon University; and Scott Hamilton, also of Brandon University. Barry Kaye, Department of Geography, University of Manitoba, and Lionel Dorge, executive director of the Société Historique de Saint-Boniface, took the time to answer specific requests, as did Garron Wells and Lucille Lang of the Archives of Manitoba, and Helen Pawsey of Hudson's Bay House.

The contribution of Warren Clubb of Saskatchewan is acknowledged separately in "A Note on the Trail." Other Saskatchewan residents who gave time and attention to my inquiries are Douglas Bocking, Jean Goldie, D'Arcy Hande, and Edwin C. Morgan of the Saskatchewan Archives Board at Regina and Saskatoon, and Ian S. Dyck, supervisor of archaeological research for the Department of Culture and Youth.

In Alberta, well-known historian and author, J.G. McGregor, and E.O. Drouin of the Oblate Archives, deserve special thanks, as do Hugh Dempsey and Lynn Huhtala of the Glenbow-Alberta Institute, A.D. Ridge of the Archives of Alberta, and Rory Flanagan, who is super-intendent of Jasper National Park and president of the Jasper-Yellowhead Historical Society. Georgeen Barrass of the Glenbow Museum and J. Blower of the Archives of Alberta assisted with research on photographs and drawings.

In British Columbia, I am much indebted to Trevor Schubert of Kamloops and to Mary Balf, curator of the Kamloops Museum; to Frances Woodward and Maureen Wilson of the University of British Columbia Library; and to Ronald and Linda McMicking of Victoria, whose help is separately acknowledged in "A Note on the McMicking Family." Thanks are due also to Terry Eastwood and Kathryn Bridge of the Archives of British Columbia, John Shephard of the Vernon Museum and Archives, and Canon Cyril Williams, archivist, Anglican Provincial Synod.

Jane Fredeman, Senior Editor, and Ryszard Dubanski, of the University of British Columbia Press, have been encouraging and helpful editors.

Finally, I am happy to thank some relatives and personal friends who assisted in most important ways, from caring for my children, to editing, researching, and typing, to exploring parts of the Overlanders' trail with me. They include my mother Rona, my sisters, Beth, Janice, and Allison and Mike Halko and Lynda Bess. Nicholas and Paula also deserve thanks for taking a lively interest in this project and for spending so many quiet hours while their mother worked.

INTRODUCTION

Thomas McMicking was the elected leader of the largest single group of people ever to cross what is now the Canadian prairie and travel through the Rocky Mountains to British Columbia before the building of the railway.[1] This group, together with three smaller parties of men who completed the same journey later in 1862, became known as the Overlanders. They were on their way to the Cariboo district where gold had been discovered in large quantities the preceding summer.

McMicking wrote an account of the trek, and his narrative was carried in the New Westminster *British Columbian* in fourteen instalments between November 1862 and January 1863.[2] The appearance of the present book marks the first occasion that the series has been collected and published in full.

There are nine extant first-hand accounts of the Overlander expeditions, not including those contained in letters.[3] Four are continuous narratives and five are diaries. Two of the accounts have been published in abridged form in this century, but only one is generally available,[4] and it was written by a member of one of the later parties.

A comparison of McMicking's text with the others, both published and unpublished, reveals that his is the best-organized, most comprehensive, and most accurate. Along with his concise and polished style, these qualities make *Overland from Canada* the most useful and readable primary source of information about the Overlanders.

The Cariboo gold rush which brought Thomas McMicking and his companions to British Columbia had its beginning in the stampede to the Fraser River in 1858. Gold had often been found earlier in small quantities in British territory north of the 49th parallel and west of the Rockies.[5] Vancouver Island, the Okanagan Valley, the Queen Charlotte Islands, and the Skeena and Thompson Rivers were all among the sites named. In 1855 a small rush was triggered at Fort Colvile on the Columbia at the mouth of the Pend d'Oreille River. Miners from this

The Trail of the Overlanders of 1862

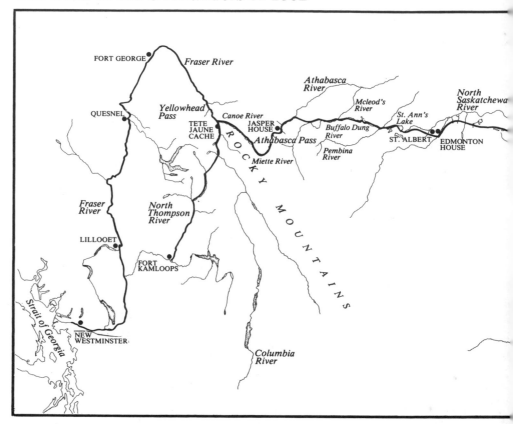

Sources: The route shown was determined from TM's notes on the trail. The map is based on
             *A General Map of the Routes in North America Explored by the Expeditions under
             Captain Palliser, during the Years 1857, 1858, 1859, 1960.* London: Stanford's Geo-
             graphical Establishment, 1865.

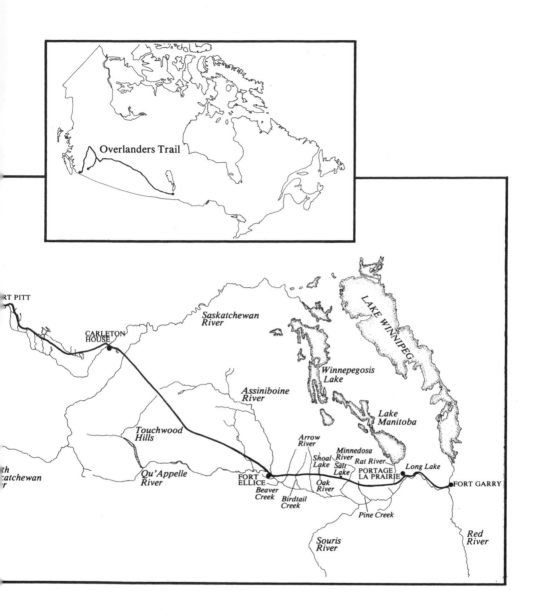

area, most of them Americans, pushed north and west to the Thompson
River. Working down this stream to its mouth on the Fraser and north
and south along the bars of the latter, they found gold in encouraging
amounts. The Hudson's Bay Company, which had a trading monopoly
in the region, exported three hundred ounces of the metal between
October and the end of December 1857. In April 1858 James Douglas,
governor of Vancouver Island, wrote to the Colonial Office in Britain
about the developments, mentioning a figure of eight hundred ounces,
"almost all the gold . . . hitherto exported from the country."[6]

Some of this gold went to San Francisco, the location of the nearest
mint. Rumours of wealth on "Frazer's" and "Thompson's" Rivers and
in the "Suswap" region were circulating in California as early as
January 1858, when the *San Francisco Bulletin* and the *Daily Alta
California* began printing articles from correspondents in Washington
territory and on Vancouver Island.[7] Infrequent at first, these reports
became a flurry during April 1858. They excited great interest in the city
which had mushroomed a decade earlier as the economic centre of the
great California gold rush.

In California, according to historian Andrew Rolle, "probably more
rich ore [had been] found near the surface than in any comparable
mining area in the world."[8] Although returns from placer deposits
(those containing loose gold mixed with sand, earth, or gravel) had
fallen off after production worth no less than $80,000,000 in 1852,[9] other
forms of mining were developed and proved profitable, and the population of the state continued to rise, to 380,000 in 1860.[10] The overflow of
this vast reservoir of ambitious people, including unknown numbers of
British, Chinese, Australian, and Canadian nationals as well as Americans, and totalling between twenty and thirty thousand men, surged
northward to the Fraser River in the spring and summer of 1858.

British Columbia's gold production, though substantial, was never
to compare with California's, but this fact was not known at the time.
Rumour had it that the Fraser strikes would prove richer than any in the
United States.[11] It was almost inevitable that such high expectations
would be disappointed. Most of the miners travelled by ship to Victoria
and there built or hired boats to take them up the navigable lower part of
the river, but about eight thousand travelled overland through the
Oregon and Washington Territories, crossing the boundary into the
Fraser Valley or moving up the Okanagan or Columbia river systems.
The Fraser itself rises late in the year compared with southern streams,
and in late May, June, and July, by the time the largest number of men
got to it, its productive bars were under water and could not be worked.
About nine of every ten miners returned home disgruntled before
autumn, complaining of the "Fraser River humbug." Those who stayed
were rewarded: gold exports from Victoria rose from $45,000 in August

to $243,000 in October.[12] These returns were solid enough to keep the most determined men in the country through 1859, and they explored far up the river, to points beyond Fort (now Prince) George.

The arrival of so many foreigners among the small white population ended the trade monopoly of the Hudson's Bay Company and forced the birth of a new colony, British Columbia. James Douglas gave up his duties as chief factor of the company but continued as governor of Vancouver Island and assumed the governorship of the mainland colony as well. He took immediate steps to establish British authority firmly and to improve communications, especially by roadbuilding. His work helped prevent the absorption of British Columbia by the United States, a very real threat in his mind in view of what had happened earlier in the Oregon region when American settlers moved in in large numbers and made it first *de facto,* and then *de jure,* U.S. territory.

There were no significant new gold discoveries in British Columbia until the fall of 1860, when a few miners exploring in the region of the Quesnel River, some four hundred miles from the lower part of the Fraser, found good placer deposits north of Quesnel and Cariboo Lakes, on Antler and Cedar Creeks. Other men attracted by this news discovered Williams Creek, the richest of all the streams in the soon-to-be famous Cariboo district, in February 1861.

The wealthiest claims, such as those of Billy Barker and John Cameron and their partners, were not staked until the summer of 1862, but by the end of 1861 the "gold product of Cariboo . . . was estimated by the *Victoria Daily Press* at $2,000,000, and by the *London Times* correspondent at $2,291,409."[13] There were about fifteen hundred people in the Cariboo region at the time, and the population swelled to five thousand the following year.[14]

In Cariboo, almost all the deposits of easily excavated placer gold, which could be separated by panning or by a simple system of sluices and rockers, were quickly staked. Miners who arrived in 1862, unless they were unusually lucky or wealthy enough to hire labourers to work the dry, deep bench claims, became labourers themselves. Many gave up and returned home within a few weeks or months, but these sobering facts were not widely circulated outside British Columbia until the end of the season.

It appears that a series of letters written in the winter of 1861-62 by Donald Fraser, the *Times* correspondent referred to above, was responsible for inducing large numbers of British subjects to start planning a journey to Cariboo in the spring. Fraser

> pictured the discoveries and excitements of the preceding year in somewhat roseate but not overdrawn coloring. [He] simply omitted the dark side of the picture; and he was particularly blamed by the

English arrivals for speaking prematurely of the stage-coaches on
the proposed wagon-road [from the lower Fraser to the Cariboo
region], when it appeared, to their grief, after travelling 7,000 miles,
that a walk of 400 or 500 miles farther, carrying a load, would be
necessary to finish the journey.[15]

The seven thousand miles to which Hubert Bancroft refers was the
distance of the Panama route to Victoria. For Canadians, this route
involved travelling to New York, taking one or several steamers to
Colon, travelling on the Panama Railroad across the Isthmus, taking
another steamer from Panama to San Francisco, disembarking and
boarding yet another for Victoria—in all, six to eight weeks' travel. The
chief disadvantage of the Panama route was its expense, in the range of
three to four hundred dollars. There was also a risk of illness: malaria
and other tropical diseases were endemic in the region.

Despite these drawbacks, most gold seekers chose the Panama journey. There were alternatives. The most adventurous and least impatient
travellers could still make the long sea voyage around Cape Horn or
through the Strait of Magellan. It was expensive and time-consuming,
so it was not a popular choice in 1862, although thousands of those
bound for California a decade earlier had come "round the Horn."

A third possibility for Canadians who wished to get to British
Columbia was to undertake an overland journey through American
territory. A westward migration of U.S. citizens to California and
Oregon had been going on for years. Well-worn trails branched from
Missouri, one southwestward to Santa Fe, and another, the famous
Oregon Trail, northwestward following the North Platte and Snake
Rivers to the Columbia. There were many hazards along the route,
including deserts, scarce feed for draught animals, the real threat of
Indian attack, and mountain passes higher than those in British
territory. Perhaps the main advantage for Cariboo-bound travellers fell
to the few who took the northern spur to the Columbia region. By
entering British Columbia in the Kootenay or Okanagan districts, they
avoided the worst of the trails along the Fraser and Thompson River
gorges.

For most other travellers, there was a choice of two paths from
Victoria to the mouth of the Quesnel. After a boat trip across the Strait of
Georgia and up the wide lower Fraser, a water and wagon route led from
the mouth of Harrison River into Harrison Lake and up to Port
Douglas, thence overland to steamers on Lillooet Lake, Anderson Lake,
and Seton Lake, and then overland again from Lillooet to Clinton. The
journey to this point, still over 300 kilometres from Quesnel, involved
loading and unloading cargo and passengers no less than eight times.
The other route led by narrow, dangerous trails along the Fraser Canyon

and part way up the Thompson River, from where it branched north-ward to Clinton. The Royal Engineers began work in May 1862 on the most difficult sections of this path, but the Cariboo Wagon Road was not completed as far as Soda Creek until the fall of 1863. From Soda Creek the Fraser was navigable to the mouth of the Quesnel, and from this point to the gold fields there were passable trails.[16]

The difficulties and expense of the southern routes to Cariboo from Canada were great enough that it is perhaps surprising that more people did not consider making the overland journey through British territory, avoiding the hazards of the lower Fraser altogether. The $97.50 which McMicking reckons as the total cost per person for the journey from Queenston to Quesnel was unquestionably much lower than that of any other road to the mines. To an armchair traveller, it may indeed have appeared the "easiest, quickest" route, as McMicking put it. Alexander Fortune,[17] one of McMicking's company, noted also that "glowing accounts" of gold discoveries on the North Saskatchewan River near Edmonton, appearing at the time in the *Toronto Globe*, had caused many of his companions to decide to try the overland path.[18]

Whatever the considerations which motivated them, a number of independent groups in Canada East and Canada West began planning overland expeditions in the late winter and early spring of 1862. They gathered by word of mouth and sometimes through newspaper adver-tisements, and there were between three and forty-five people in the several parties which assembled at such centres as Toronto, London, St. Thomas, and Montreal.[19] Thomas McMicking was the leading or-ganizer of the Queenston or St. Catharines company, which included about twenty-four men and which was from the beginning one of the most strictly disciplined units. Two other members were Robert Burns McMicking, Thomas's younger brother, and Samuel Chubbuck, his brother-in-law.[20]

Thomas McMicking "the Sixth," as family papers designate him, was the oldest son and second child among twelve born to Mary (née McClellan) and William McMicking. He was born on 16 April 1829, in Stamford Township, Upper Canada, at the farm which his paternal grandfather, Thomas McMicking "the Fourth," had established about 1783 after coming to Canada from the Delaware River after the Revolu-tionary War. Born in Scotland, grandfather Thomas was a Loyalist, as was Mary McClellan's father, John. Both men had received grants of land in the Queenston district; the McMicking farm was situated on the bank of the Niagara River, "about a mile from the historic little village of Queenston."

Despite this Loyalist background, as Victor Hopwood has pointed out, the political outlook of Thomas's immediate family may have been Reformist. In a biographical sketch of Robert Burns McMicking, published in 1890 in Vancouver, J.B. Kerr stated that Robert's "first impressions in political ethics were formed in the William Lyon Mckenzie [sic] school."

Thomas received his early education in Stamford. Later he may have studied at Toronto's Knox College. Always a religious man, he was ordained an elder of the Presbyterian church in Stamford in 1854 at the age of twenty-five. In the same year he married nineteen-year-old Laura Chubbuck, of Queenston, and they soon became parents: Thomas, Jr., was born in 1856, Laura Augusta in 1857, William Francis in 1860, and Robert Lincoln in 1862, after his father left for Cariboo.

Following his marriage Thomas continued working for a short time on his father's farm. He then taught school briefly at Queenston and in 1856 went into business there in partnership with one of his wife's relatives. In 1861 he ran for election at Niagara as the Clear Grit candidate, but he was defeated by his Conservative opponent John Simpson. His business as a "general dealer" never prospered, although he continued in it until his departure for British Columbia.[21]

This summary suggests that by 1862 McMicking still had not established himself to his own satisfaction in any profession. It was a time when some ambitious men were beginning to feel crowded in Canada West. Most of the good farmland had been pre-empted or was available only at a high price from speculators who had bought up the Clergy Reserves. Commercial ventures were risky in the sluggish economy which followed the railway-building boom of the 1850's. The news from Cariboo made it seem "alike the duty and interest," in McMicking's phrase, for those of a certain adventurous temperament to seek to provide for their own and their families' futures in the west. Alexander Fortune had time to reflect, as he journeyed toward Detroit on the first stage of the overland trek, that "range after range for many miles deep Ontario's habitable lands were occupied, and that her sons would year after year follow me and others to the west not finding scope near home to satisfy their longings."[22] The biographical evidence indicates that most of the Overlanders were young men from farming families. Some were immigrants brought by their parents from Ireland, Scotland, and England. A few had schoolteaching experience, and more had experience in business, most often as clerks. A handful had some training in the professions.

The Queenston party left St. Catharines on 23 April 1862, and McMicking's narrative begins with a description of the journey to the Selkirk Settlement via Windsor, Detroit, Milwaukee, La Crosse, St. Paul, Georgetown, and the Red River. By the end of May nearly two hundred Canadians had arrived in Fort Garry. They were as yet organized in small groups only, but after several days of discussions and practical preparations, a majority of the men agreed to leave on 2 June and proceed to Long Lake about two and one-half days' travel on the trail along the Assiniboine River. There they stopped for final organization. McMicking states that his large party eventually included about one hundred and fifty people when all stragglers had arrived.

Popular histories of the expedition have sometimes assumed that all the Cariboo-bound overland parties of 1862 travelled with McMicking, but this was not the case. Those left behind at Fort Garry after 2 June set out several days later in two separate contingents. One group of twenty was led by an American doctor named Symington.[23] Up to now very little has been known about this party, but information recently discovered in the Hudson's Bay Company's 1862 Fort Edmonton Journal has shed a little more light on its activities.[24] Another unit numbering sixty-three, some of whom had originally belonged to the group organized by a police sergeant named Stephen Redgrave at Toronto, is usually known as the "Redgrave party."[25] It was actually commanded from Fort Garry to Edmonton by an American adventurer named Timolean Love and two very capable half-breed guides, John Whitford and George Flett.[26] Neither of these companies managed to overtake McMicking's, although the Redgrave party intended to do so. The diarist Richard Alexander and the artist William G.R. Hind, whose illustrations are included in the present publication, travelled from Toronto to British Columbia with Redgrave. The story of this company is told in more detail below in a note on W.G.R. Hind.

There was yet a fourth party of Overlanders in 1862, composed of five men from London, Canada West, and called the "Rennie party" because it contained three brothers of that name. This group did not arrive in Fort Garry until after the McMicking, Symington, and Redgrave companies had departed. The story of the Rennies and their friends, which was not known to McMicking when he composed his narrative, and which is not mentioned in the basic history of the expeditions, M.S. Wade's *Overlanders of '62*, is a harrowing one of death by starvation, exposure, or murder in the wilderness above Fort George in the winter of 1862-63—and of cannibalism.[27]

All three of the companies which left Fort Garry after McMicking's suffered more disorganization and hardship than the leaders. This observation raises the question of what information McMicking and his followers had about the route and the preparations they would have to make before their departure.

British North America west of the Selkirk settlement was a trading preserve of the Hudson's Bay Company at the time. The region was not well known, but two expeditions, one led by Captain John Palliser for the British government in 1857 and 1858 and another headed by Henry Youle Hind for the Canadian government in the same years, had recently reported on the suitability of the prairies for settlement. Hind's

*Narrative of the Canadian Red River Exploring Expedition of 1857, and
of the Assiniboine and Saskatchewan Exploring Expedition of 1858* was
published in London in 1860. In 1862 Hind published at Toronto a
small volume entitled *A Sketch of an Overland Route to British
Columbia.* It is not clear if any of the Overlanders read this book before
they left their homes in the east, but a comparison of McMicking's
description of his party's timetable and outfit with Hind's advice on
these matters strongly suggests the possibility.

Hind recommended that overland travellers gather at St. Paul or St.
Cloud in American territory not earlier than the last week in April. If
carts and horses or oxen were to be used from this point, the journey
should not be begun before the second week in May, for all streams
would be flooding and there would not be sufficient grass for fodder.
The Métis, he noted, travelled this route no earlier than 1 June annually.
If "connections were properly made," the journey from Toronto to Fort
Garry should not take longer than twelve to thirteen days. At Fort Garry,
if not before, the small Red River carts made entirely of wood should be
purchased, together with extra axles. Heavier wagons could not be
extricated from deep mud or sand or manoeuvred as easily. With regard
to draught animals, Hind noted that horses were faster but not as strong
as oxen, while mules were hard to find. Hind went on to detail the kinds
and amounts of food needed, as well as other equipment. Two oil-cloths
were absolutely necessary, as well as an india-rubber or gutta percha
cloth "for crossing rivers," and each traveller must have one complete
change of good strong clothing, plus flannel shirts, worsted stockings,
and flannel drawers. A tent, however, was not essential.[28]

On 28 May 1862, the *Fort Garry Nor'Wester* published an article
entitled "Information for Miners." It recommended, "Professor Hind
being the authority," a more southerly route than the one later actually
followed by the Overlanders, describing a path from Fort Ellice along
the Qu'Appelle, to the Elbow of the South Saskatchewan, on to
Chesterfield House, the Red Deer River, Old Bow Fort, and through the
Rockies via "Kananaski" or Vermilion Pass. The article was continued
in the 11 June issue of the paper, with information from Palliser's
expedition, but by then McMicking's party had left Fort Garry. In any
case, neither the Palliser nor the Hind report contained good information on the route via the Yellowhead Pass and beyond, which was the
most direct though not the easiest or safest path through the mountains.

McMicking makes it clear that he and his companions waited until
they were actually in the country to seek detailed information about the
route. At the Hudson's Bay Company posts from Fort Garry on, they
spent much time in consultation with traders, trappers, and guides, and
they hired guides when they could. Supplies, however, were not so easily
obtained, so it is fortunate that Hind, or some equally competent

authority, had advised the Overlanders on what to purchase before they set out. There are few complaints in any of the accounts about a lack of essential equipment, although unexpected delays caused most of the men to run short of food in the mountains. On the other hand, as McMicking noted, their "mining tools ... were the only articles ... found to be unnecessary."

The purpose of the organizational assembly at Long Lake, which took place on the morning of 5 June 1862, was to draw up travelling rules and to choose a leader for the journey ahead. Details from other accounts reveal that George Wallace, a "correspondent from the *Toronto Globe*," acted as secretary while crouched on the ground.[29] The chairman, Thomas McMicking, sat on a water cask.[30] His name was one of three put forward for leader; the other two are not recorded. When the vote was counted, it was unanimous for McMicking.

Most of the Overlanders had not had much time to get to know Thomas McMicking. That they so unhesitatingly placed their confidence in him at Long Lake indicates that his good character and leadership abilities must have been quite striking, even on short acquaintance. An incident which occurred in May while the Canadians were in camp at Georgetown illustrates McMicking's qualities of decisiveness and diplomacy.

Alexander Dallas of the Hudson's Bay company unexpectedly arrived at the Minnesota outpost on his way to take up his duties as governor of Rupert's Land.[31] As Robert McMicking's diary shows, on hearing the news, his brother quickly organized about seventy of the "Cariboo boys" to march to Dallas's residence "in double file." The men fired a salute into the air for the governor. Afterwards

> The Captain [Thomas McMicking] then Introduced Himself and the Company, The Governor then thanked the Company & Introduced a Hiland piper who played two or three tunes. The Co. then gave three cheers for the Governor, Three for her Majesty & for the President of the U.S. Three for the piper and again Three for the Governor & three for His Lady. The Co. then Marched back to Camp Singing God Save the Queene, The piper went to the camp to[o] and gave us another tune there.[32]

This enthusiastic display netted a mark of special favour for the men who had performed it. "The governor with a few other Gentlemen were up from the town to see us tonight," Robert noted the next day. From other accounts we know that Dallas spent some time in conversation with the men and gave them information about British Columbia. According to A.L. Fortune, he also agreed to send a courier ahead of the Overlanders to ensure the co-operation of the HBC employees at the posts along the way.[33] No doubt there were other early occasions when Thomas McMicking took action which convinced the "Cariboo men" that he would make the best leader, though no specific ones have been recorded.

The rules and style of organization adopted at Long Lake by the Overlanders were almost military. In American territory, some of the California-bound overland parties had adopted "elaborate rules and regulation, uniforms, and even a bugler."[34] The earliest American travellers also postponed choosing a commander until they had been a few days on the trail. Possibly a few of the men in McMicking's company had first-hand experience travelling with American wagon trains. McMicking briefly mentions "some Californian miners who accompanied us," and A.L. Fortune relates that his friend James Wattie, who had been in California a few years before, was able to communicate (in pidgin English) with Chinese gold-panners on the Fraser River for that reason.[35]

A true military order was not possible for the Overlanders, any more than it had been for most of the American caravans, whose members displayed a marked "propensity to amend rules, depose leaders, and reshuffle companies en route."[36] But although McMicking's group did amend a few rules governing the daily schedule, they did it amicably, and there is no hint in any of the accounts of serious dissatisfaction with the leadership, nor were there any desertions from the ranks. One of the reasons for this harmony appears to have been that McMicking and his committee "lieutenants" allowed their followers a good deal of latitude. The young men from Huntingdon, Canada East, as described by John Sellar,[37] sometimes ignored the regulation that each of the smaller parties making up the large brigade should take turns at the head of the cart train.[38] In the morning Sellar and his friends would rush to get ready and start first, denying the others a chance at a relatively unrutted trail, the pick of wild game, and the choicest camping spot at night. McMicking's committee handed out some reprimands but chose not to expel the offenders from the caravan. The wisdom of this restraint became clear later at the most difficult sections of the trail, when the eager Huntingdon crew forged ahead building bridges and hacking a path through the tangle of undergrowth.

McMicking's level-headedness is evident in his assessment of the threat of Indian attack. While at least a few of his followers foresaw terrifying encounters on this journey to "the far North West, where the Redmen of the forest goes prowling about at all hours, waiting for an opportunity, when an inocent white may fall into their power, in order to shed his blood & feast upon his flesh,"[39] McMicking calmly recorded that "we were informed that should they make any demonstrations it would be more likely for the purpose of stealing our animals than with any design against our persons." One of the rules made at Long Lake had been that all dealings with Indians en route were to be conducted through the captain and the guide. This rule seems to have been adhered to, with good results. At different times, native people supplied the party with food, transportation, and goods such as buckskin clothing and moccasins. After the trip was over, McMicking judged the "red men of the prairies to be our best friends," and noted that "before we reached the end . . . we were only too glad to meet with them."

McMicking does not stress the importance of his role as leader, but he makes it clear that important questions were decided in consultation with all those who had information to contribute. The success of this democratic process was partly the result of the generally high level (for the time) of education among the men and partly of their consciousness of the dangers of disunity, but it also came from McMicking's political tact and understanding, sense of justice, and administrative ability.

McMicking and his committee encouraged certain social activities which fostered a feeling of community among the travellers. These functions included musical evenings, when all gathered to sing or to listen to the members of a "Musical Association" play fiddles, flutes, and horns. Even more important, certainly in McMicking's view, were the regular Sunday rest and religious services. Many of the Overlanders were pious Protestants; a few, such as Catherine Schubert, the only woman in the company, were devout Catholics.[40] Their faith, as their leader indicates, provided them with a common set of values to which they could refer when friction developed, and it helped them accept with courage the deprivations and tragedies of the latter part of the journey.

Mention of the only woman Overlander touches upon an aspect of the saga which has attracted a great deal of attention. In his narrative, McMicking has little of a personal nature to say about many of his companions, but near the end he pays a generous tribute to Catherine Schubert's courage and maternal devotion. Mrs. Schubert and her husband Augustus were living at Fort Garry with their three small children when the Canadians arrived there in 1862. Augustus Schubert decided to join the miners, and his wife, although pregnant with a fourth child, refused to be left behind. A number of later histories claim that before leaving the settlement the Overlanders relaxed their rule against women for her sake. In fact, the rule is not stated explicitly in any of the accounts. A.L. Fortune wrote simply that it was never the "intention" of the party to include families. Fortune's narrative suggests, and Schubert family tradition holds, that the young parents with their offspring and two young French-speaking attendants did not catch up with McMicking's company until it had travelled some distance from the settlement. Presented thus with a *fait accompli* at White Horse Plain or at Long Lake, the committee may only then have decided to accept the

Schuberts. The presence of the family does not appear to have caused any delay or inconvenience on the journey. Some of the young men helped carry the children over dangerous and awkward terrain and at river crossings, and in Fortune's words, "the kindly sympathy of many of our men was frequently manifested to the heroic woman and her small children. . . . Her presence in the company helped to cultivate a kindly and more manly treatment of man to man."[41]

This considerate treatment of the Schuberts illustrates the spirit of reasonableness and co-operation which generally marked the actions of the members of McMicking's party in spite of their numbers, the stresses of the journey, and the impatience felt by many to get to Cariboo at all costs before the mining season ended. Fortune, again, aptly noted that his companions consistently displayed "a spirit of order where the law of the land could not punish."[42] Their consideration extended to their animals, about whom there are numerous expressions of concern in all the accounts. Perfect harmony did not always prevail: some verbal disputes and one fist-fight, which, as Fortune lamented, "we grieved to see," are reported. On the whole, however, the record indicates that a thoroughgoing decency was one of the outstanding characteristics of the Overlanders as a group and that much of the credit must go to their leader, "one of the finest men I ever saw," as McMicking was described by a close companion.[43]

Much has been said about McMicking's virtues, and it balances the picture to report that he possessed a few faults. In one or two places his narrative reveals a tendency to an almost Calvinistic harshness in judging others. One such passage includes a passionate denunciation of the conduct and character of Charles Rochette, a guide who deserted the Overlanders near the Qu'Appelle River.[44] Rochette, a Métis, had been recommended by the Roman Catholic bishop (later archbishop) of St. Boniface, Alexandre Taché.[45] McMicking alleges that some of his companions conjectured that Rochette and Taché had conspired to cheat the Overlanders. The ludicrousness of such charges, considering Taché's reputation, did not deter McMicking from dignifying them by inclusion in his published account.

Rochette may not have deserved the "universal execration" called down upon him. There is some evidence in the other journals that conflicting demands were secretly pressed on the guides by different factions among the trekkers who wished to obtain special privileges.[46] Since Rochette forfeited half his payment by deserting the Overlanders, he may have had a reasonably strong motive for doing so.

McMicking's role as leader of the expedition terminated at Tête Jaune Cache on 1 September. Here, after leaving Fort Edmonton and crossing the Rockies through Yellowhead Pass to the headwaters of the Fraser, the trekkers held a meeting to dissolve their committee. They had built rafts and canoes to float down the river to Fort George and embarked the same afternoon. A small group of about thirty-six, including the Schubert family, agreed to take most of the remaining pack animals and try to cut a trail overland to the North Thompson River and along it to Kamloops. They left the Cache on 2 September.

McMicking's account ends with the arrival of his own party and some of the other rafts and canoes at the mouth of the Quesnel River, the entrance to the Cariboo district, on 11 September. He adds a postscript describing the trials of the Thompson River travellers, with details obtained from some of the men who had proceeded from Kamloops to New Westminster in late autumn.

Very few of the Overlanders actually saw the Cariboo goldfields before the summer of 1863. Many, exhausted by their ordeals and disillusioned by the reports of experienced miners returning through Quesnel, simply walked down to the coast and took ship for home immediately. Others wintered at New Westminster or Victoria and returned to Cariboo in the spring. A considerable number stayed in British Columbia but never mined. They went on to find prosperity and contentment in more secure occupations.

Thomas McMicking, his brother Robert, and his brother-in-law Sam Chubbuck were among the few who did visit the goldfields at Williams Creek for a few days in September 1862. Finding no prospects there, they returned to the Fraser and worked their way down to New Westminster where they laboured for a time in a shingle-mill.

Probably McMicking soon found more congenial employment.[47] He may have been befriended by John Robson, the controversial editor of the *British Columbian*, who later became premier of the province. In any case, Robson—who helped a number of other Overlanders during the first lean days at New Westminster—agreed to publish McMicking's narrative of the journey as soon as it was finished.

It is not known what McMicking did for a living until 1864, but clearly he was not idle. In the three and one-half years following his arrival in New Westminster, he took part in public affairs of all sorts, as president of the Temperance Society, volunteer in the Hyack Fire Company,[48] elder of St. Andrew's Presbyterian Church, and president of the local Bible Society. He became a member of the hospital board and was listed as auditor of the British Columbia Coal Mining Company, whose directors included John Robson and Joshua Homer. He was a member of the school committee and secretary of the British Columbia Mill Company.

Early in 1864 McMicking welcomed his wife and children to the west, and in the same year he was appointed town clerk and assessor for New Westminster, at a salary of $750 annually. In 1865 the McMicking's fifth child, another son, was born. A few months later news of the Fenian raids in the east prompted organization of a Home Guards unit in the city, and McMicking became a senior lieutenant. In April, 1866, Joshua Homer, high sheriff of the colony, appointed him deputy sheriff for the district.[49]

McMicking's life was cut short a few months later, on 25 August 1866, when his second son Frank, then six, fell into the Fraser River during a family visit to friends who lived about eleven kilometres below the city. Thomas went to the boy's rescue, but they were both swept under a log boom and drowned.[50] McMicking's funeral was the largest ever seen in New Westminster to that date. At a memorial service held a few days later, the pastor took for his text a verse from the 37th Psalm: "Mark the perfect man, and behold the upright, for the end of that man is peace."

With his vigour, talent, and ambition, no doubt Thomas McMicking would have played a significant part in the business and political life of British Columbia if he had lived longer. Other Overlanders went on to become prominent citizens and collectively contributed much to the development of the new province. John Mara, for example, had a highly successful business and political career.[51] He started out with a small store at Seymour Arm on Shuswap Lake about 1864, then went into the freighting business on Kamloops Lake and the North Thompson River. By 1882 he controlled a steamboating company, had stores and real estate at Kamloops and Sicamous, and owned interests in the Shuswap Mill. Later he became a chief shareholder in the Shuswap and Okanagan Railway Company. As a politician he served as MLA for Kootenay, a large riding which included most of southeastern British Columbia, and in 1883 became speaker at Victoria. In 1886 he was elected Conservative MP for the federal riding of Yale-Cariboo and served until his defeat by Hewitt Bostock in 1896. He was noted as a champion of Confederation.

Another Overlander, John Fannin, originally a schoolteacher from Kemptville, C.W., was one of those who actually mined in Cariboo for several years.[52] Later he pursued a varied career as a shoemaker, taxidermist, big-game hunting guide, and surveyor for the provincial government. He was passionately interested in natural history, and he possessed a "choice collection of birds and animals." This collection came with him when he moved to Victoria after Premier Robson appointed him first curator of the Provincial Museum in 1886. According to Fannin's obituary in the _Colonist,_ his aptitude for natural history amounted almost to genius, and his work was recognized across the continent.

There is not space here to describe in detail the successful careers of other Overlanders who remained in British Columbia, but they include Alexander Fortune, lay missionary and first settler in the North Okanagan Valley; Richard Alexander, manager of the Hastings Sawmill at Vancouver and alderman and founding father of the city; William

Fortune (no relation to Alexander Fortune), pioneer businessman and farmer at Kamloops;[53] John Bowron, after whom the Bowron Lakes are named and who spent many years in the Cariboo district as mining recorder, government agent, and gold commissioner;[54] and G.C. Tunstall, who held similar posts at Granite Creek, Revelstoke, and Kamloops.[55] Details of Robert McMicking's successful career in telegraph, telephone, and electrical companies are given in the "Note on the McMicking Family."

The Overlanders were but a handful of the thousands of men who were attracted to the Cariboo from the Orient, Europe, and especially the United States, but they are important because they acted upon a vision of Canada as one land "from sea to sea" before the nation became a political reality. McMicking shows himself to be clearly aware of this aspect of their achievement in the eloquent plea for Confederation with which he concludes his narrative.

Overland from Canada has literary as well as historical value. McMicking's style is smooth and balanced, with a clarity we associate with a more experienced author, yet as far as is known he wrote nothing else for publication. He packs much information into a small space, and this compact manner is well suited to the description of a long journey with myriad details of scene and incident. A discussion of geological phenomena in the Rockies, a passage of theological reflections, a quotation from Pope's *Essay on Criticism,* another from Charles Wolfe's "Burial of Sir John Moore at Corunna" are a few of the indications of the quality of his education, which speaks well for the standard of schooling in Canada West in the mid-nineteenth century.

McMicking's plot naturally possesses the universal appeal of an adventure story. It is a romance in which ambitious youths ride off in search of treasure and on their way must overcome a series of formidable difficulties. Against an alternately idyllic and nightmarish wilderness backdrop, McMicking's real-life heroes perform feats of daring, endurance, and self-sacrifice. One such incident ended in the death of Arthur Robertson.[56] McMicking first sets the scene by describing the menace of the Fraser River's Grand Canyon. He then relates the story of the canoe accident and Robertson's brave but futile battle to swim to shore and get help for his friends. Finally McMicking pays tribute to Robertson's character in terms in keeping with Christian and chivalric ideals.

Although McMicking tends to emphasize the practical possibilities of the wilderness through which the Overlanders passed, his narrative contains numerous lyrical descriptions of the natural world, revealing that he well understood the Romantic distinction between the sublime and the beautiful. The tamer kind of loveliness was to be found on the prairies and particularly in the fertility and promise of the valley of the

North Saskatchewan, which had the "fitness and capacity for becoming the homes of a dense population." But the vast, rugged Rocky Mountains were sublime beyond all expectation and aroused deep religious feeling, exemplified in the description of the thunderstorm at the camp on the Athabasca River near Roche Miette. McMicking was not alone in his awe; similar testimony can be found in almost all the Overlander accounts. Their experiences in the mountains were never to be forgotten, and are of enduring value. For many Canadians today, too, the appeal of the wilderness varies in proportion to the amount of solitude and wild grandeur there—in short, with its sublimity, although the word has lost the power it had in McMicking's time.

In spite of a general sobriety of character and style, McMicking did not lack wit or a sense of humour. He regales us with descriptions of several comic scenes from the march, such as the chaotic crossing of the Pembina River west of Edmonton, when he rises to heights of mock heroic eloquence.

McMicking's work falls into a category of exploration and journey writing which is well represented in Canada's literary tradition. The diaries and narratives of such western travellers as David Thompson, Alexander Mackenzie, Paul Kane, and Walter Cheadle are just beginning to receive attention for their literary merits. Like McMicking's, these accounts describe expeditions into little known territory and share the basic plot of the classic tale of action. They are full of fascinating details and curious anecdotes and possess according to the varying abilities of their authors more or less drama, poetry, and psychological interest. Those who have enjoyed any of these better-known works, and many other readers as well, will find McMicking's narrative entertaining as well as informative.

William G.R. Hind: The "Expedition Artist"

The illustrations for this book include the attractive and informative paintings and drawings of William George Richardson Hind (1833-89).[1] Hind was an Overlander, and some of his works have been used to illustrate popular histories of the McMicking company's journey. However, Hind did not travel westward from Fort Garry with McMicking but with the so-called Redgrave party. This group travelled between one and three weeks behind McMicking's and, in fact, followed a different trail at times.

Hind's work, never well-known, was almost completely forgotten until J. Russell Harper began bringing it to public attention a little over a decade ago. Hind left a number of finished paintings as well as a notebook, now in the Public Archives of Canada, containing close to one hundred sketches and water colours relating to the overland journey. These constitute a unique and valuable record; yet the sketchbook was until recently attributed to W.H. Ellis,[2] another member of Redgrave's party who took Hind's notebook with him when he returned to the east by way of Panama in May of 1863. It is only since Harper's early investigations that the painter's connection with the Overlanders has been clearly established. The present publication of McMicking's narrative marks the first occasion that Hind's illustrations have appeared with any of the original accounts of the expedition, and a number of the scenes included here have never before been reproduced. Hind's choice of subjects and the care with which he depicted them indicate that he was conscious of the historical value of his record, although his nationality and what we know of his character make it unlikely that he was very interested in the political questions to which McMicking on occasion directs our attention.

At the time of the Cariboo expedition, Hind was twenty-nine years old and a bachelor, as he remained until his death. Very little is known about his early years except that he came from a respectable English manufacturing family. He had followed his older brother, Henry Youle

Hind, who had emigrated to Canada in 1846 (and later became a well-known surveyor, geologist, editor, academic, and author), to Toronto around 1851. William set up a studio and also taught painting and drawing at the Toronto Model School, but he does not appear to have had much success selling or exhibiting his work in that city. His later painting shows some influence of the English Pre-Raphaelite movement, particularly in its stress upon detailed, almost scientifically accurate depiction of subjects and also in his use of vivid yet delicate clear colours, but it is not known where or with whom he studied.

In 1861 he returned from a trip to England in time to accompany his brother Henry, who, as noted above, had earlier been a leader of Canadian government exploring expeditions in the prairie region, on yet another government-financed exploration up the Moisie River from Sept Iles to Labrador. When H.Y. Hind's report, *Explorations in the Interior of the Labrador Peninsula*, appeared in 1863, it contained many woodcuts and coloured lithographs by William. Knowledge of his part in this project may have prompted recent suggestions that he was appointed "official artist" to the Overlanders, but in fact he seems to have been considered only another of the many gold seekers. Few if any of his companions even thought to mention that he was a painter, and Wade overlooked the fact in the *Overlanders of '62*. McMicking's reference to "our special artist" in his description of the Pembina River crossing in August 1862 appears to have been purely hypothetical. On that day Hind was still one hundred and fifty miles east of the river with Redgrave's party.

The full story of Hind's company is to be found in *The Diary and Narrative of Richard Henry Alexander in a Journey across the Rocky Mountains*, published in 1973 by the Alcuin Society, and also in Alexander's unpublished journal and papers and in the unpublished journal and papers of Stephen Redgrave, all in the Provincial Archives of British Columbia.

It was at one time the intention of Hind and his companions to winter east of the Rockies and do some prospecting on the North Saskatchewan and Bow Rivers; but for various reasons, chiefly lack of supplies and better intelligence regarding the improbability of finding paying prospects in Alberta, about half of Redgrave's group, including Hind, carried on through the Yellowhead Pass in September, eventually reaching Fort George about the beginning of October.

Hind shared a tent with Richard Alexander and Alexander's friends John Carpenter and Alf and Henry Handcock on the trip from St. Paul into the Saskatchewan country. But as they neared the south branch of the river on 9 July, trouble which had apparently been brewing for some time came to a head, and Hind was asked to leave Alexander's "mess." "There has," wrote Alexander, "been so much ill-feeling in our tent

Plate 1. Duck Hunting on the Prairies. Many of the Overlanders were keen hunters; Hind paints one bagging supper for the wagon train of travellers in the distance. His meticulous attention to detail shows in the markings of the dead mallards at the hunter's belt. AC

Plate 2. In the Leather Pass. A resting point on the tortuous climb through the pass. Though some of the Overlanders persisted i
using donkeys, horses and even oxen as pack animals, many of the men carried 50-60 lb. packs as they crawled along the precipitou
trail. Now there were few with energy to appreciate the view that only days before had astonished them.   PABC

Plate 3. Pine Forest, B.C. An ox labours to clamber over fallen pines and poplars, a far cry from the proud and confident animal that crossed Saskatchewan pulling a wagon loaded with 800 lbs. of supplies. Stephen Redgrave, organizer of Hind's group, credits the Huntingdon party with clearing a way through the interminable forest.   McCord Museum, McGill University, Montreal

Plate 4. Saloon with a Group of Men on the Fraser River, B.C. Lillooet, as the Overlanders would have seen it, with bleak mountains in the distance and saloons lining the main street, is typical of the towns the miners visited. Inside the saloons, the successful swapped lies and drank while their exhausted fellows slept on the floor, their packs for pillows.   McCord Museum

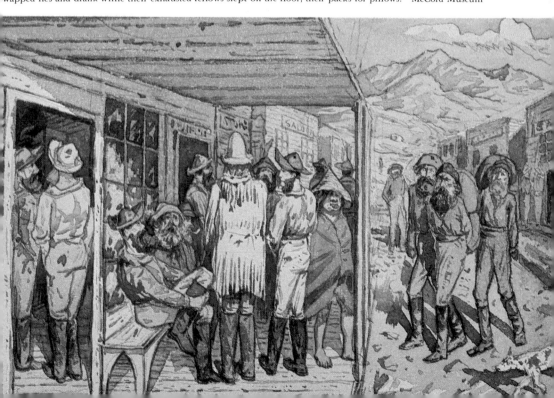

Plate 5. Chinese Gold Washers on the Fraser River, B.C.: "These were the first mining operations we saw" TM says of a group of Chinese gold washers above Quesnel. Often the Chinese repanned the streams to find small nuggets left by Europeans who had rushed on the new fields and greater wealth.   McCord Museum

Plate 6. Fraser River, B.C.: "So placid indeed was the stream . . . that we were induced to float all night" wrote TM after a fearsome struggle with rapids and rafts on the Fraser. Here an open valley allows the river to flow unimpeded and serene over glacial till.   McCord Museum

between Hind, and I may say all of us except Alf, that I had to tell him that he would have to leave us and that we would divide with him fairly."[3] A day later Hind and Stephen Redgrave began sharing a tent.

The nature of those of Hind's traits and habits which prompted this rift is never mentioned. From other sources, it is known that he was often taciturn, though "a good talker, when inclined to be communicative," and of "grand and occasionally eccentric habits."[4] The only clear impressions to emerge from the written record of the expedition—apart from Alexander's hint that he was difficult to get on with—are that the artist was an enthusiastic hunter and at times also an enthusiastic drinker. Redgrave's party, though smaller than McMicking's, was not as tightly organized and suffered throughout the trip from more dissension, changes of plan, and "splits in the ranks." Drinking and gambling were not unheard of, and before the departure from Fort Garry such activities occasioned some criticism from one or two of McMicking's men.[5]

The "Toronto" people also moved at a more leisurely pace, stopping frequently to prospect or hunt. An interesting sidelight to their story is that as far as Carlton House, Hind's party was accompanied by the wonderful Felix O'Byrne (or O'Beirne), that learned buffoon, garrulous divine, and slothful coward whose story is so entertainingly told in Milton and Cheadle's *North-West Passage by Land* and Cheadle's *Journal.* Apparently realizing what a burden O'Byrne would be on the journey through the mountains, the party arranged to leave him at Carlton, from where he made his way to Edmonton by the time he met Cheadle in May of 1863.

From Fort Garry to the crossing of the South Saskatchewan, all the Overlanders followed essentially the same route; but at that point Redgrave, Hind, and their companions turned southwest to below the Elbow of the North branch (whereas McMicking's brigade crossed the river at Carlton and cut across country past the Thickwood Hills to Fort Pitt). In the vicinity of the Eagle Hills south of the river, Hind and his group were overjoyed to find buffalo in abundance. (McMicking's men, also eager to hunt, had not seen any of the great beasts, being left "sore at heart at the sight of bones only," as A.L. Fortune put it.)[6] Somewhere east of present-day Two Hills, Alberta, just after crossing Vermilion "Creek," Hind's party again struck the "regular trail to Edmonton"— that is, McMicking's trail—"little else than a series of marshes, mud holes and creeks to that Fort, which we reached August 8th,"[7] according to Richard Alexander. Several members of the group departed at Edmonton, travelling south to the Bow. Hind, Alexander, and Redgrave carried on with about twenty-two others along the trail to Jasper. By the time they got to the high country, their provisions were nearly exhausted and winter was coming on. There was no grass for the animals and the trail was in places a quagmire. Fortunately, McMicking's men had passed that way only about a fortnight earlier and with great labour had hacked away the worst of the brush and bridged many swamps and streams. Without their work, as Redgrave generously acknowledged,[8] it is likely that his group would have been so seriously delayed as to have lost some members to starvation and exposure. In his diary, Alexander tells how at one point he and several friends spent two days without food on the trail to Tête Jaune Cache.[9] The Shuswaps camped near the Cache enabled them to get their strength back by providing salmon, berry-cakes, and small game.

Hind and his companions proceeded to build rafts and canoes, just as McMicking's men had done a few weeks earlier. Again the canoes proved a poor choice. On 30 September Alexander nearly lost his life and his friend Carpenter was drowned at the same spot where Robertson had died three weeks before and where more recently another companion from Fort Garry to Tête Jaune Cache, Philip Leader,[10] had been lost. Unfortunately, it is not known how Hind made his way to Fort George, because his tent-mate Redgrave stopped keeping his journal on 21 August, but in a letter written years later Redgrave stated that the length of the journey from the Cache to Fort George was fifteen days. Since Alexander and three companions were the last of the group to reach the HBC outpost, on 8 October, having been delayed by their accident, we can assume that Hind arrived a few days earlier. On 24 October Alexander noted in his diary that he had caught up to Redgrave at Bridge Creek near Lac la Hache, but he did not mention Hind, though the artist may have been one of the "lot of others" staying in a shanty there.[11] The last mention of Hind occurs in Alexander's journal entry for 22 November 1862 (but not in the published version of Alexander's diary and narrative, which is abridged): "I have met the Meaford fellows. They are making shingles just opposite our shanty [near New Westminster]. Purdy, Fife, Hind, and Coffering, Wright and Collins, are down at Frisco."[12]

In spite of the rigours of the trip, Hind found plenty of time to sketch, at least until the party entered the mountains. The sketchbook shows no scenes dated later than 29 August 1862—the last is a view of the Rockies from somewhere just beyond the McLeod River—but several finished paintings depict parts of the route beyond that point as far as Yellow-head Pass, and J.R. Harper reports the existence of one painting of a Shuswap dwelling at Tête Jaune Cache, now in the McCord Museum at Montreal.[13]

The selection of Hind's illustrations for the present book has been guided by the documentary rather than the artistic quality of many scenes. Pictures showing activities, such as buffalo-hunting, which were not engaged in by McMicking's men, have been excluded. The decision to include a large number of rough studies rather than a smaller number of more polished works was made chiefly because what the sketches lack in polish is made up in immediacy. There is in them a strong sense of the gritty reality of a sometimes desperately difficult journey. In addition, the interested reader can now find reproductions of many of Hind's paintings in J.R. Harper's books.

Many of the sketches were given descriptive titles and some are dated, so that a number of the incidents portrayed can be located in Alexander's or Redgrave's diaries. By design, most of the scenes included in the present volume have parallels in McMicking's or his companions' narratives. They show men in the mud with their shoulders to the wheels of mired wagons; men hauling on lines to prevent carts and animals from running away down steep banks; carts loaded on the Hudson's Bay Company's scow crossing the Assiniboine; a bridge, probably originally built by McMicking's men, breaking down as Hind's companions attempt to cross it; and the first clear view of the Rockies. In fact, Hind has caught so many of the most dramatic episodes that one begins to wonder if his sitting and sketching at the most difficult moments was one cause of the resentment felt by Alexander and his tent-mates.

Animals, especially oxen, appear in over half of Hind's drawings, emphasizing the importance of the Overlanders' draught animals. In one of the liveliest scenes an ox, unaccustomed to being loaded with a pack, careens away from its hapless owner scattering goods and breaking harness. John Sellar, of McMicking's party, described similar scenes on the road between Edmonton and Lac Ste Anne as

> some of the most tyriffic though laughable sceans that I ever witnessed, & which put me in mind of tying a tin pale to a Dogs tail. . . . I believe the Oxen were still worse they would jump, kick, bellow & throw themselves down, & get up again repeat the scean, & kell over and thrash about. . . . & if loaded with baggage, they often strewed it over an acre of ground & in such a confused state that it was almost imposible for the driver to get it picked up again, while the horse & mule drivers would laugh fit to kill themselves.[14]

One of Hind's drawings shows the view from above and behind an ox which is pulling a cart on the rolling prairie—obviously executed from the driver's seat and portraying what was certainly one of the most familiar sights on the trip. Other studies include a close-up of a pack-saddle, and another of the yoking system used on the oxen; a lovely view of the animated faces of Hind's friends in "Tales over the Campfire"; and quick but accurate impressions of vegetation along the route, from a young poplar on the Saskatchewan to spruce forests on the eastern slope of the Rockies. They illustrate Hind's attention to detail, which gives much of his work a strongly documentary quality.

Those finished scenes which have been included in the present book illustrate aspects of McMicking's journal which the sketchbook does not cover such as a view of Yellowhead Pass, or as Hind called it, the Leather Pass, from a high trail and Chinese gold washers on the Fraser River, which, though probably painted some years later, shows these workers and their methods and tools as McMicking's people must have seen them in 1862.

Whether or not Hind visited San Francisco in November 1862, by February of 1863 he was in Victoria and had established himself in business as an artist. Very little more has come to light about his stay in British Columbia. Over the next few years he made at least one and possibly several trips back to the interior to record life in the Cariboo and on the trail to the goldfields. Paintings from this period, many of them now in the British Columbia Archives and in the McCord Museum at Montreal, convey a feeling for the daily "grind" of the prospectors' work as well as for the dingy crowded accommodation and the boredom of life in the camps. Hind sensitively caught the oppressively masculine atmosphere, from which the miners themselves sought distraction in liquor and in endless card games.

Sometime toward the end of the decade Hind left Victoria and returned to the east. Either on his way or shortly after arriving he paid an extended visit to Red River again and made some fine studies of winter life in Manitoba. He moved to New Brunswick at the end of 1870 and spent most of the rest of his life there, working for some years for the Intercolonial Railway, possibly as a draftsman, and painting and sketching for his own pleasure.

In his introduction to J.R. Harper's text in the catalogue[15] of an exhibition of Hind's paintings at Windsor in 1967, Kenneth Saltmarche praises the artistry in Hind's "sensitive and creative brush," in his "coloration," and in his "very personal way of seeing and drawing." These tributes apply particularly to Hind's finished work. But the critic also points out that the pictures have "as their first and most immediate appeal the attraction of the historical document." This assessment is especially true for the scenes done on the spot during the trek. For those interested in the history of the west as well as those interested in the history of the Overlanders, there is much to study in the selections from Hind's wonderful pictorial diary of 1862. They form the visual counterpart of McMicking's narrative.

A Note on the Text

The only extant version of Thomas McMicking's narrative of the overland journey of 1862 is contained in a series which was originally published in the New Westminster *British Columbian*. The fourteen instalments of the account appeared in the newspaper on the following dates: 29 November 1862; 3, 10, 13, 17, 20, 24, 27, and 31 December 1862; and 10, 14, 17, 24, and 28 January 1863. No other published or unpublished letters, diaries, or papers written by TM have been discovered. Excerpts from the *British Columbian* series are included in many histories of the Overlanders, but the entire account has never before been collected and published in one volume.

TM composed his narrative of the journey while its scenes and incidents were still fresh in his mind, but it is clear that he did not rely on his unaided memory for the many precise details he includes. He may have been able to refer to his brother Robert's personal diary of the trip, but this is not certain. Evidence in Robert's journal indicates that TM set out for New Westminster from the upper country on 28 September 1862, leaving Robert working as a cook for a roadbuilding crew near Bridge Creek. Neither Robert nor, presumably, his diary reached New Westminster until 16 November, several days after the date of composition (10 November) indicated in the first instalment of TM's narrative. Moreover, TM mentions the "scrupulous care with which a record of our daily progress was kept," and such a description does not apply to Robert's journal, which, although valuable, is sketchy in parts.

It is probable that TM himself, as leader of the expedition, kept the detailed record of the trip to which he refers. It may have been included in a personal diary which has since been lost. There is one clue pointing to the existence of such a document. In an article entitled "The Overland Journey of the Argonauts of 1862" (*Proceedings and Transactions of the Royal Society of Canada*, 3d ser., 13 [1919], p. 37), F.W. Howay mentions that he made use of the "original diaries" of Robert McMicking and of "his brother, Thomas R. McMicking. These little books," Howay states, "contain a day by day account of the incidents of the whole journey." But the quotations in the article are taken from Robert McMicking's journal alone, and later Howay refers repeatedly to "the diary" (singular). It may be, then, that Howay was using Robert's journal together with TM's published account and refers loosely to both as diaries.

There is a possibility that another version of the published narrative once existed. In his introduction to the 1973 reprint of Margaret McNaughton's *Overland to Cariboo,* which was first published in 1896, Victor Hopwood discusses the evidence. It occurs in a passage quoted without attribution by Mrs. McNaughton in her book:

> A brief description of the making of pemmican may be quoted here as of possible interest to the reader. It was made from the flesh of the buffalo and was very nutritious. "As soon as the animal is killed the lean flesh is separated from the fat and cut into strips, which, after being roasted over the fire, are thoroughly dried in the sun. The meat, being by this time very hard, is spread out on the skin of the animal and beaten with flails until quite fine. The fat is then melted, and about sixty pounds poured into a bag containing about forty pounds of lean meat. The fat and lean are then thoroughly mixed and left to cool, when all is ready for use. It becomes very hard; in fact, it has to be cut with an axe" (p. 24).

As Dr. Hopwood notes, this passage is very close to the description of the method of preparing pemmican contained in TM's narrative, but it is also "sufficiently different that the discrepancies can hardly be ascribed to simple misquotation. Also, the final statement about pemmican becoming so hard as to require an axe to cut is not to be found in the printed McMicking account" ("Introduction," *Overland to Cariboo,* p. 6). Dr. Hopwood concludes that this evidence raises the question of whether Mrs. McNaughton was in possession of an unedited draft of TM's narrative or, perhaps, his personal diary.

The text of the account as it appears in the *British Columbian* presents certain editorial problems. The general policy has been to preserve as nearly as possible what TM actually wrote. There are numerous typographical errors in the newspaper series. It is obvious, for example, that he did not write *Irodhois, contiderable,* or *thrritory.* Such mistakes have been silently corrected. Where TM uses a form which was once accepted but is no longer current, as in *Hudson Bay Company* or *sulphurious,* his usage has been retained. Where two different spellings of the same word appear in the original text, as in *Frazer/Fraser* or *Queenstown/Queenston,* the more modern or correct form has been preferred throughout.

Many punctuation faults in the original appear to be printer's errors.

For example, full stops appear in the middle of sentences, or are omitted or replaced by commas at the end. Such mistakes have also been silently emended.

There are very few paragraph divisions in the original text, and some of those fall where there seems to be no break in the sense. They have been eliminated and new divisions added where it seemed necessary. The purely arbitrary divisions between instalments in the original have also been eliminated.

TM sometimes spells personal names incorrectly. In the case of well-known historical figures, the correct spelling has been added in square brackets the first time the name appears, and after that TM's form is used without comment. The same practice has been followed where TM's spelling of his companions' names differs from that used in the standard history of the expedition, M.S. Wade's *The Overlanders of '62.* Dr. Wade's forms have also been preferred in the editorial material in the present book, with the exception of TM's brother-in-law, Samuel Chubbuck. Dr. Wade obtained his information from documents and sources close to the other Overlanders, and research indicates that his forms are usually correct.

TM's variants of place names and some Indian words have been retained without comment in all cases where he was consistent and the modern spelling is sufficiently similar that the reader will have no difficulty recognizing the term. Otherwise the modern spelling or name has been added in square brackets the first time the word or phrase appears.

In a few instances, words have been added to sentences for the sake of clarity or grammatical correctness. These additions also appear in square brackets.

TM often capitalizes "River," "Valley," "Pass," etc., in place names, but sometimes does not. In the present edition, all such parts of place names have been capitalized. Capitals have also been added at the beginning of direct quotations where TM or the printer originally omitted them. On the other hand, TM in common with other nineteenth-century authors sometimes uses capitals where they would be omitted today, as in *this Country* and *the Eastern World,* and these appear unchanged in the present book.

Apostrophes have been added in possessives. Where TM uses italics for emphasis, no change has been made. Italics, rather than McMicking's quotation marks, have been used in printing the names of steamboats. A line of poetry, set between quotation marks and appearing in reduced type in the original, has also simply been italicized here.

The spelling of French words, names and phrases has been regularized: *bateau* instead of *batteaux, Tête Jaune Cache* instead of *Tête-jeune-cache,* and so forth.

Quotations from the unpublished papers of other Overlanders and from unpublished documents such as HBC journals have been included in the editorial material. The spelling and grammar of these excerpts is often erratic. Editorial devices such as [*sic*] and other parenthetical explanations have, however, been used as little as possible, in order to avoid a cluttered text. I hope that the liveliness and personal flavour thus retained will make up for any inconvenience to the reader.

"*Then Canada, our home, with her golden fields, and Columbia, the land of our adoption, with her fields of gold, shall become one and the same country, indissolubly united by a common nationality, and cemented by a community of commercial interests—one of the strongest links in that chain which binds together the great brotherhood of nations.*"

Thos. McMicking, 1862

AN ACCOUNT OF A JOURNEY OVERLAND FROM CANADA
TO BRITISH COLUMBIA DURING THE SUMMER OF 1862,
EMBRACING A GENERAL DESCRIPTION OF THE COUN-
TRY, TOGETHER WITH THE VARIOUS INCIDENTS, DIFFI-
CULTIES AND DANGERS ENCOUNTERED; FOR
CIRCULATION IN THE EASTERN BRITISH COLONIES. BY
MR. THOMAS MCMICKING, OF QUEENSTON, CANADA
WEST.

To the Editor of the British Columbian

New Westminster, B.C.
November 10th, 1862

DEAR SIR,———Since the rich discoveries of gold in this Country have
invested every thing and every place near it with new interest, and have
turned the attention of the Eastern World to consider the easiest,
quickest and cheapest road for reaching it, a description of the Overland
Route, as we found it, may not be uninteresting to your readers here, and
through your exchanges to the people of the East. I purpose then, with
your permission, to give through your columns a few particulars of our
journey, together with a description of the country through which we
passed, the difficulties we overcame, the dangers we escaped, the losses
we sustained and other matters connected with the route.

The party with whom your correspondent was more immediately
connected was organized at Queenston, C.W., and consisted of the
following twenty-four men, viz: Archibald Thompson, Stratford; John
Bowland [Boland], Queenston; F.C. Fitzgerald, St. Catherines; James
Willox, St. Davids; Leonard Crysler, Niagara; Joseph Robinson,
Queenston; Robert Brownlee, St. Catherines; Robert Harkness,
Iroquois; I.D. Putnam, Ingersoll; James Rose, St. Davids; William
Gilbert, Queenston; Dobson D. Prest, Queenston; Thomas Murphy,
Stamford; R.H. Wood, Niagara; A.M. Connell, Queenston; John
Hunneford [Hunniford], St. Catherines; Simeon E. Cummer, St.
Davids; Samuel W. Chubbuck, Queenston; W.H.G. Thompson,
Niagara; John Fannin, Kemptville; Robert McMicking, Stamford; W.
Fortune, St. Davids; Peter Marlow, Queenston; and Thomas McMick-
ing, Queenston.[1] Our personal outfit, varying of course according to the

judgment or fancy of the individual, and the cost of which will not be reckoned in our list of expenses, consisted generally in one good strong suit, from three to six changes of under-clothing, a pair of knee boots and a pair of shoes, a rubber coat and a pair of blankets; and [we were] armed with a rifle, revolver and bowie knife. Besides these every one was provided with a few drugs and patent medicines, and such other little articles as each considered necessary.

Thus equipped, after bidding an affectionate farewell to the "loved ones at home," we started on our hazardous and difficult journey on the 23rd day of April last. Our party were in the best possible spirits, and full of bright hopes for the future. We left St. Catherines by the Great Western Railway at 11:40, A.M., and arrived at Windsor, 229 miles from home, at 10, P.M. We had taken the precaution to provide ourselves with a certificate from the Custom House at Queenston, and armed with this we had no difficulty in transporting ourselves and our goods into Uncle Sam's dominions. We crossed over immediately to Detroit where we remained until the next morning, the 24th. At 10:15, A.M., we left Detroit by the Detroit and Milwaukie Railway, and arrived at Grand Haven, on Lake Michigan, 186 miles from Detroit, at 8, P.M. Here we took passage immediately by the steamer *Detroit,* and arrived at Milwaukie, 86 miles from Grand Haven, at 2 o'clock on the following morning. Here we stopped until 5 o'clock, P.M., when we left by the Milwaukie and Lacrosse Railway and arrived at Lacrosse on the Mississippi River, 201 miles from Milwaukie, at 10 o'clock, P.M., on the 26th, having been detained eight hours by a break in the railway, 4 miles from Portage City. At Lacrosse we embarked on board the steamer *Frank Steele*,[2] and at 2 o'clock began the ascent of the "Father of Waters." The Mississippi was at this time very high and overflowed a great extent of country on both sides of the river. We ought to have reached St. Paul on the night of the 26th, but owing to sundry delays, whether accidental or intentional, we did not arrive until 10 o'clock on the evening of the 27th.

Although at so great a distance from them that it is only just possible that it will reach them or the public who travel by that way, yet I must be allowed, on behalf of our party, to enter my protest against the treatment we received from the officers of the *Frank Steele.* By an arrangement with the railway managers, in consideration of the number of our party, we were furnished with through tickets to St. Paul, securing to us first class accommodation, at second class rates. We had been treated with uniform courtesy by all parties until we went aboard the boat; but here we were crowded together between the decks, where we had no room to lie down, and refused provisions, although we offered to pay for them, what ever they might ask.

When we left home we did not know that we should have the

company of any others besides our own party; but upon arriving at St. Paul we found a great many from different parts of Canada already there, and others continually coming, upon a common errand with ourselves. We found St. Paul a thriving city.[3] Here we purchased our groceries, mining tools, tents, dishes, &c. Our course from St. Paul was by Burbank & Co.'s stages to Georgetown on the Red River;[4] and from the limited accommodation for carrying passengers, and the great number wishing to go, we did not leave St. Paul until the 2nd day of May. Our first day's drive brought us to St. Cloud on the Upper Mississippi, 77 miles from St. Paul. This is a busy little town, and growing rapidly. Some of our company bought their flour and bacon here for the journey. The next day we drove 62 miles and camped for night at Sauk Centre, a stage station on Burbank's road. The country on the road from St. Paul to this point is a beautiful rolling prairie with occasional strips of wood-land, is tolerably well settled, and appears to be a good farming county. The farmers were just sowing their spring crops as we passed through. The climate was becoming sensibly colder as our course was nearly due north, and during the next day we passed several small lakes covered with ice, and heavy banks of snow were still lying along the sides of the hills. We camped for the night at Pomme-de-terre, 63 miles from Sauk Centre. The next day's drive brought us to Graham's Point, on Red River, 55 miles from our last camping place. Here we had to remain until Wednesday the 7th of May, as we had overtaken some of those who started before us, and the stage could not carry us all at once. We then started again and drove to Lewiston, another station on Red River, having only made 38 miles. The next day brought us to Georgetown, 25 miles from Lewiston, and 320 from St. Paul. Georgetown is situated on the Red River, at the present head of steam navigation, and only contains a tavern, a storehouse belonging to the Hudson Bay Company, a residence for the H.B. Co.'s agent, a barracks for about 30 U.S. soldiers, and one or two other small houses—all of logs.[5]

Before leaving home we had made enquiries from Messrs. J.C. Burbank & Co., the proprietors of the boat, respecting the navigation of the Red River, and were informed that the new steamer *International*[6] would positively leave Georgetown, on her first trip for Fort Garry, on the 10th day of May, and we timed our arrival there accordingly. But to our great disappointment upon reaching Georgetown we found that the boat was not yet finished. While we were waiting for the boat Governor Dallas of the Hudson Bay Company, with his family, on their way to Fort Garry, arrived at Georgetown. He visited our camp there, gave us much valuable information respecting the country thro' which we were intending to travel, and kindly offered to do what he could to assist and protect us while within H.B. Territory.[7] I cannot allow this opportunity to pass without thus publicly thanking the H.B. Company, and particularly Governor Dallas, for their uniform kindness to our party while on their way.[8]

During the time we were waiting at Georgetown parties for the overland trip to British Columbia were continually arriving, so that by the time the steamer was ready to sail about 150 were on hand. We did not leave Georgetown until the 20th day of May, having waited there twelve days. The water in Red River at this time was unusually high, with strong currents setting across the points among the timber. The boat being somewhat unmanageable, it was found impossible to keep her in the channel, and we had not gone more than two miles before she ran among the timber, tearing down both her smoke pipes and damaging her slightly in other respects. This was rather discouraging after waiting so long, but it was only the beginning of our troubles on the Red River. This was about 2 o'clock on the afternoon of the 20th, and the boat was not ready to sail again until 10 o'clock of the 21st. At this time we started again, but had only gone a short distance when, at 3 o'clock, the engine gave out. This being repaired, we made a short run before dark, when, as usual, we tied up for the night. On the morning of the 22nd the wind blew pretty strong, and Capt. Noble did not think it advisable to sail before 4 o'clock, P.M. About 7 o'clock, in backing up to turn one of the short bends, she ran against the bank and damaged her wheel, so that another delay was necessary. The 23d was passed with accident.

The 24th, being Her Majesty's birth-day, was celebrated on board the *International,* although within United States territory, by raising the Union Jack, firing a salute, and by a social dinner, at which toasts, speeches and songs were the order; and the manner in which the celebration was received proves the deep attachment of Canadians, under all circumstances, to our Gracious Sovereign. On the 25th we were delayed two hours by a break in the rudder, and reached Pembina, near the boundary line, at 3 o'clock in the afternoon. Here we stopped for a short time, and at 5:30 we crossed the 49th parallel and entered the British Possessions. During the day we passed several groups of Indians, who greeted our approach by firing guns, shouting, running, jumping, and other violent gesticulations. These demonstrations were interpreted by some as signals of welcome; by others as tokens of hostility and defiance. From the tragic scenes that have recently been enacted in that neighborhood,[9] it would seem that the latter opinion was correct, although they were probably prevented from making an attack by the presence of so many armed men on board.

On the morning of the 26th we were informed that we were fifty (50) miles from Fort Garry by land, and about 110 miles following the course of the river, and that we should reach the fort during the day. This information appeared to infuse new life into the company, and to revive

the spirits of those who had already begun to despair of ever reaching the
end of a journey so inauspiciously begun. All parties were accordingly
early on the move, arranging baggage and freight for unshipping, or
keeping a keen lookout for the expected fort. We met the first portion of
the settlement about 30 miles above the fort. At 4 o'clock in the afternoon
we sighted the fort,[10] from which a salute was fired, as the boat entered
the mouth of the Assiniboine, in honor of the arrival of the new steamer,
and bidding a kindly welcome to the "overlanders." As the vessel neared
her moorings the salute was answered by a volley from about 150 rifles
on board the boat. It appeared as though all "Selkirk," by whom our
arrival was expected, were there, in their holiday attire, to receive us; and
it was an occasion that will long be remembered by them, as inaugu-
rating a new era in the history of the colony.[11] I ought to have stated that
Governor Dallas did not wait for the boat at Georgetown, but proceeded
overland on horseback, accompanied by Mr. McKay, the celebrated
guide;[12] and, reaching Garry before us, had announced our coming and
made preparations for our reception. We were honored with the
company of Lady Dallas down the river.[13] We landed at 5 o'clock, having
been over six days in making what ought to have been accomplished in
two.

Upon reaching the fort we found that, with those who had come
down the river in canoes or overland, besides residents of the settlement
who were intending to go with us, our company was increased to about
200 souls. Our next business was to gain all the information possible
respecting the trails across the plains, and the different passes over the
mountains, as we had not yet fully decided which pass we should take.
For this purpose we had frequent meetings and consultations among

Camp at Fort Garry

our own company, and several interviews with Governor Dallas; Mr.
McTavish [Mactavish], master of Fort Garry; Mr. Christie, master of
Edmonton, who happened to be in the settlement; Bishop Taché;
Timoleon Love, who crossed the mountains from this country in 1860;
John Whiteford [Whitford?], the guide, and others.[14] After much
deliberation it was agreed to make the Edmonton House our next point,
and leave the selection of the route beyond until we should know more
about it from the people living there.

We now discovered that the delays we had suffered hitherto were
rather an advantage than otherwise, and that our only mistake was in
leaving home by three or four weeks too early, as the feed on the plains
would not have been sufficiently up to have allowed us to have left Fort
Garry sooner. Our next care was to procure a guide upon whom we
could rely, and as we had so often heard of parties being deserted by their
guides in different places, we determined to approach the subject with
very great caution. In pursuance of this plan, we made an engagement
with one Charles Rochette, a French half-breed, to conduct us to the
Edmonton House; and, as he was strongly recommended by Bishop
Taché as a trustworthy guide, we supposed we had secured the very man
we wanted; but with what results the sequel will show.[15] We were to pay
him one hundred dollars for his services, one-half of which was
deposited with the Bishop, to be handed to Rochette when he should
return with a certificate from us that he had fulfilled his engagement;
and the balance was to be paid him upon our arrival at Edmonton.

In the meantime some of our number were engaged in purchasing
horses, oxen, harness, provisions, and such things as were necessary to
complete our outfit. This was in some cases a rather slow operation, not
that there was any scarcity of the articles in the settlement, but the extraordinary demand induced many of them to ask more than we considered
them worth. We succeeded in buying horses at an average of about forty
dollars each, oxen thirty dollars, carts eight dollars, and harness four
dollars. There were a few very good animals among the horses, but the
majority were of a very ordinary description. Oxen were however more
generally used, and we found them all noble animals, possessed of great
endurance, and rapid travellers. The Red River carts were odd looking
affairs, constructed wholly of wood, without even a nail for a fastening,
and, before we became accustomed to their appearance, were the
occasion of many a joke. The harness is made of raw buffalo hide, and
served a very good purpose while we kept it dry, but was somewhat
troublesome on account of its stretching if it happened to get wet.

Our provision consisted chiefly of flour and pemican, which we
bought principally from the Hudson Bay Company at the rate of $3.90
per 112 lbs. for flour, and six cents per lb. for pemican. The flour, which
was manufactured in the settlement, was a good, sound, wholesome

article, but somewhat dark and coarse. From the samples of wheat that we saw, the produce of the colony, with proper mills number one flour ought to be made. Pemican is prepared buffalo meat, and is made in the following manner: as soon as the animal is killed the lean portion of it is separated from the fat, and cut into thin strips, which, after being roasted over the fire, are thoroughly dried in the sun until they become quite hard and brittle. It is then spread out on the skin of the animal and beaten with flails until it is quite fine. This is then put into sacks made of

Drying Buffalo Meat

the green hide, with the hair side outward, and containing about one hundred pounds, and the fat, after being rendered, is poured over it while hot. The bag is then firmly sewed up, and the pemican is fit for use. Although not a particle of salt is used in its preparation, it will keep in this way for years. But few of our party could eat it at first, its very appearance and the style in which it is put up being apt to prejudice one against it; but all by degrees cultivated a taste for it, so that before we reached the mountains it not only became palatable but was considered, by most of us, an absolute luxury. It is the principal, and in many cases the only food used by the employees of the Hudson Bay Company, and, indeed, by all the inhabitants of that territory, and is found to be wholesome and nutritious, and admirably adapted to the country.

We found the Red River Colony a considerable settlement, extending along the banks of the river from about thirty miles above Fort Garry to the mouth of the river, and along the Assiniboine westward for about twenty miles. It contains some ten thousand inhabitants, the great

majority of whom are half-breeds. The settlement is under the government of the Hudson Bay Company, and the administration of their laws
appears hitherto to have given general satisfaction. But the time has
arrived when they are no longer suited to the necessities or desires of the
people, and they are earnest and united in their appeals for the
establishment of some kind of responsible government in which they
can have a voice. They demand that the Imperial, or Canadian,
Government shall open up for them some better communication with
the rest of the world; and, from the strong feelings so freely expressed to
us upon the subject, it is very evident that, unless something be done to
change their circumstances, they will seek some other national
relationship.

The soil appears to be well adapted to the production of nearly all the
cereals and vegetables common to the temperate zones; but one is
forcibly struck while passing through the country by the indifferent
manner in which it is cultivated, or rather by the total want of
cultivation. This unsatisfactory state of affairs is induced by the want of
a market for their surplus produce, when they have any, by the absence of
all competition, and by the ease with which they can obtain a subsistence
without labor, the rich plains affording unlimited pasturage for their
herds.

But let them be supplied with a market such as they had for the short
time that our party remained with them, and the country would soon
present a very different aspect. Society there seems to be in a sort of semi-
organized condition, and a great many remains of Indian customs and
practices are observable in the habits of the people; indeed it is said that
the Indian manners are rather being revived.

From the difficulty experienced in procuring an outfit for so large a
party, our start from Fort Garry was likely to be delayed considerably if
we waited until every one was ready; it was therefore agreed that as each
separate party were ready they should move slowly on in order to obtain
good feed for their animals, that they should rendezvous at White Horse
Plains, 25 miles from Garry, and there wait for the balance of the
company and be prepared to start from that point on Thursday morning
the 5th of June. On Sabbath, the first day of June, religious services,
specially arranged for our company, were held in the Court House at the
fort, and were conducted by the Rev. G.O. Corbet [Corbett], of the
English church, in the afternoon, and by the Rev. John Black, of the free
Presbyterian church, in the evening.[16] Both these services were peculiarly interesting and appropriate, and very acceptable to the company.
An unusual excitement was produced in our camp this afternoon, by a
person shouting from the bank of the Assiniboine that a man was
drowning in the river. We at first supposed that it must be some one of
our own company who had incautiously ventured beyond his depth

On the Trail

while bathing, and everyone rushed to the scene of the disaster, each anxiously enquiring after the other, when it was ascertained that the unfortunate man was one Anderson, a servant of the Hudson Bay Company.[17]

On Monday the 2nd day of June, at 5 o'clock in the afternoon, according to our arrangement with other parties, we started from Fort Garry, having one ox and cart for every two men, and each loaded with about 800 lbs. We found this rather too heavy a load for our animals where ever the road was rough and hilly, and especially towards night, after a long day's drive, although they could draw it with apparent ease upon smooth and level roads. About 600 lbs. would have been sufficient both for the comfort of the animals and the safety of the cart. Our course was nearly due west from Fort Garry, the trail following up the Assiniboine, but generally at some little distance from the river.[18] The Assiniboine, which flows into the Red River at Fort Garry, is a considerable stream, and is navigable for small craft for some distance above Fort Ellice. Its waters, which are very muddy and run with a strong current, have worn for themselves a deep channel in the soft and mellow soil through which they flow. It, in common with most of the streams in that territory, is bordered by a strip of timber on each side, consisting chiefly of poplar and elm. During the day we passed several very comfortable residences, two of which, namely, those of Mr. James McKay, the guide before mentioned, and John Roan, his brother-in-law, would be a credit to any country. But few of the inhabitants speak the English language; and our attempts to gather information from them were frequently frustrated on that account. They represented the season as being unusually dry and unfavorable for the growth of their crops, which appeared to be about as far advanced as the same crops would be in Canada about the middle of May. They consisted principally of oats, barley and spring wheat. We camped the first night at Sturgeon Creek, 7 miles from Fort Garry. Here we found abundance of feed for our cattle.

We started the next morning, the 3d, at 9 o'clock, having been delayed until that hour in searching for some of our horses which had strayed some distance from our camp, and halted for the night at 6:30, at White Horse Plains, where there is a trading post of the Hudson Bay Company.[19] As this was the place of rendezvous agreed upon, we remained here until 3 o'clock, P.M. on Wednesday, when but few of the parties having arrived, it was thought advisable to move slowly on a short distance further. We were informed by our guide that we would find water about 3 miles from White Horse Plains, and we determined to drive to that point and camp for the night. Not dreaming that there could be any mistake about this information, we did not take the precaution to fill our water-kegs before starting, and having driven seven or eight miles without finding water, it became a question whether we should go on or retrace our steps to White Horse Plains. After some consultation we decided to proceed, hoping that we would soon meet with water, for as the evening was very warm both our animals and ourselves had become very thirsty.

Our road now lay across a wide, open prairie, and as it had become quite dark we were obliged to trust to our oxen to follow the trail. After travelling along in this way for some time we began to entertain serious apprehensions that we were on the wrong track, and at midnight a halt was ordered for a little, to consider what was best to be done. With many of the party the thirst had become almost intolerable, and the majority preferred enduring the fatigue of a still longer march to camping where we were without water. We accordingly moved on, and had marched a considerable distance in silence, every one bearing his trouble like a Briton, when suddenly, above the creaking of our carts, the shrill notes of the sweetest music rang out on the midnight air. It was the song of the bull-frog, that had borrowed its melody from the fact that it indicated our approach to water. These indications were soon confirmed by the welcome word from the front, "Water ahead." Upon coming up we found that we had reached Long Lake, where we camped at 2 o'clock on the morning of the 5th, and though our party were generally considered temperate at home, we might without slander be accused of hard drinking on that occasion.[20] We had travelled eleven hours without rest, and not being inured to walking, we were very tired. After coming into camp we discovered that two of our party were missing, and they did not reach our camp until 9 o'clock. In wandering in search of water they had

Tent by Long Lake

missed the track, and in the darkness of the night were unable to find it again.

As many parties had now arrived, it was considered prudent to complete our organization before proceeding further. Upon calling a general meeting it was found that the following parties and numbers were present, viz: Queenston, containing 24 men; St. Thomas, 21; Huntingdon, 19; Ottawa, 8; Toronto, 7; Montreal, 7; Ogdensburg, N.Y., 7; Red River settlement, 7, including Mrs. Augustus Schubert and three children; Acton, 6; Whitby, 6; Waterloo, 6; Scarborough, 5; London, 5; Goderich, 5; and Chatham, 3; making 136 in all; and with those who overtook us subsequently our party was increased to about 150 before reaching Edmonton. The remainder of those who were with us at Fort Garry, comprising the St. Peters, or Doctor Symington's party, the Toronto party, under Capt. Redgrave, and the Huron party, and numbering about 50 men, followed us in two companies, but neither of them succeeded in overtaking us.[21] After considerable deliberation the following regulations were adopted by the company: A captain was to be elected by the whole company, to whom was to be entrusted the general management of the train, so far as the time for starting, the order of the different parties in the train, the rate of travelling, the time for halting, the arrangement of the camp, &c., are concerned; the guide was under his special direction, and he was to be the only means of communication with the Indians, should we meet any on our way. In the discharge of these duties he was to be assisted by a committee composed of one member from each of the separate parties comprised in the company.

T. McMicking, of the Queenston party, was then chosen Captain, and the different parties were represented on the Committee as follows: Queenston, Mr. W.H.G. Thompson; St. Thomas, Mr. Hutchinson; Huntingdon, Mr. Wattie; Ottawa, Mr. Jos. Halfpenny [Halpenny]; Toronto, Mr. Wallace; Montreal, Mr. Morrow; Ogdensburg, Mr. T. Phillips; Acton, Mr. Fortune; Whitby, Mr. Simpson; Waterloo, Mr. Broklebank; Scarborough, Mr. Hough; London, Mr. Urlin, and Goderich, Mr. A.C. Robertson.[22] These matters having been arranged, it was ordered that the largest party should take the lead in the train and that the remaining parties should follow in the order of their size, that the following day the leading party should go to the rear, the second party leading, and so on in rotation until each party had its turn on the lead. The object of this order was to prevent jealousy, the first place in the train being considered the best, both for procuring game and passing over soft places in the road before it was worked up too deep by driving over it.

Everything being ready we started from Long Lake at 2 o'clock in the afternoon of the same day, with ninety-seven carts and about one hundred and ten animals, some of them being used under the saddle,

besides a few spare ones for relieving those in harness in case of accident.
So large a company made a very imposing appearance as it "dragged its
slow length along" over the plain, and when marshalled in close order
extended a distance of over half a mile. Our march was now conducted
with great regularity, and, excepting an occasional break in our carts or
harness, we had but few delays. When an accident of this kind happened
to anyone he was ordered to turn out of the train and repair immediately,

Upset

for which purpose we had provided ourselves with tools, and then take
his place at the rear of the train, so as not to disturb the order of the rest.
We camped that night about sundown, at a small lake on the open
prairie, without a single tree or bush in sight. Our guide expected to find
plenty of water here, but owing to the dryness of the season we had some
difficulty in getting enough for ourselves and our animals. Nearly all the
water we used during the first part of our journey was procured from
stagnant ponds, and very little of it was fit to be used without careful
straining and boiling.

All parties acquainted with the country, and with whom we had
conversed upon the subject, were unanimous in recommending us to use
the greatest caution, both upon our march during the day and especially
while camped at night, in order to guard against the Indians who are
continually roaming over these plains. We were informed that should

they make any demonstrations it would be more likely for the purpose of stealing our animals than with any design against our persons. Our camp was therefore arranged in a triangular shape, the carts forming a corral, being drawn up side by side with the shafts outward, and our oxen were tied inside of this enclosure, each to his own cart. The tents were then pitched on the outside, each party occupying the ground opposite to their carts. Six men were appointed to watch at a time, two being stationed on each side of the triangle. The first watch began at 10 o'clock, and was changed every two hours. During the first part of our journey the night was divided into three watches, the camp being roused at 4 o'clock so as to be ready to start at five o'clock, allowing one hour for preparing and eating breakfast. We usually drove till 11 o'clock when we halted for dinner—started again after dinner at 2 o'clock, and camped for night at 6 o'clock, making 10 hours of travelling each day. A little experience however soon convinced us that six hours drive in the forenoon without feed was too much for our cattle, and when the nights became very short we arranged it in this way. We set only two watches during the night, waked the camp at half past 2 o'clock, started at 3

One of the Ills

without breakfast, drove till 5, halted 2 hours to feed our animals and breakfast, started again at 7 and drove till 11, when we halted for dinner, making 10 hours a day as before, but [the drive] was performed apparently with much greater ease. Our average rate of travelling was about two and a half miles per hour.

On Friday the 6th we stopped for dinner at Prairie Portage [Portage la Prairie], a trading station of the Hudson Bay Company, and camped for the night at a small lake. So far our road was good, and nearly the whole distance over open prairie. The character of the country passed on Saturday was somewhat different from what we had previously seen. We crossed several small streams of clear, cold water, with high, steep banks, down which we had to steady our carts with ropes, and a few miry sloughs, where it was necessary to put our shoulders to the wheel to assist our cattle through. It was rather amusing to notice the expedients resorted to by the "boys" to obviate the necessity of going into the mud on this their first initiation into this mode of travelling, but I assure you most of us lost all delicacy upon this point before we reached the Fraser; for, after taking the trouble two or three times of stripping off our shoes and stockings, and rolling up our pants above our knees, and then going in up to the middle, we came to the conclusion that there was no use being too fastidious about the matter. The road to-day was pretty rough, a portion of it lying through the heaviest timber we had seen since leaving Fort Garry. We camped on Saturday night on the bank of Soft River, a clear, rapid little stream, with gently sloping banks and shaded at intervals with groves of poplars.[23] As the fire had quite recently passed over this locality we found the feed rather short for our animals.

The next day, the 8th, being the Sabbath we remained in camp. A special article in the constitution of our company provided that we should rest regularly on the Sabbath, unless some urgent necessity should compel an advance; and it is a source of gratification to your correspondent to be able to report that this regulation was scrupulously observed. A portion of the day was devoted to religious worship, a practice afterwards regularly observed throughout our journey. These exercises were generally conducted by Mr. Joseph Robinson, of Queenston, but on this occasion by Mr. A.L. Fortune, of Huntingdon, and consisted of prayer and praise and the reading and exposition of a portion of the Scriptures. Whatever may have been the sectarian differences that prevailed among us at home, it was gratifying to know that here we could meet upon common grounds and present our united petitions for that Providential protection we so much needed. Upon these occasions our friends at home were objects of special solicitude, and a fervent and cordial amen would burst from a hundred hearts as unnumbered blessings were invoked on behalf of the dear ones whom we had left so far behind us. While the vast and lonely plains revibrated with the notes of our songs of praise, the mind was intuitively invited to contemplation, and to enquire whether these sounds might be recognized as the footfalls of advancing civilization, or to wonder as the last echo of these unwonted sounds died away in the distance, whether eternal silence and solitude were again to succeed.

Our road on Monday was very heavy, lying mostly through strips of deep yellow sand. At 10 o'clock we crossed the Points Creek, 110 miles from Fort Garry.[24] Shortly after leaving our camp on Tuesday morning the 10th, we came to a beautiful creek, but with soft marshy banks, which detained us about two hours in crossing.[25] The weather up to this time had been exceedingly dry and warm, but a slight thunder shower at 1 o'clock had the effect of materially lowering the temperature. We passed to-day through what our guide called the mountains. They were nothing more however than would be considered in Canada gently undulating lands. We camped this night on the margin of a beautiful little lake, with which this section of the country abounds. At 10 o'clock in the forenoon of the 11th we reached the Little Saskatchewan [Minnedosa River], a branch of the Assiniboine.[26] This is a fine stream, about forty feet wide, and from three to four feet deep at our fording place. Its banks are about two hundred feet high, and enclose a valley of unsurpassed beauty and fertility, stretching away to the right and left as far as the eye can see, and clothed with a rich covering of grasses, fresh and rank in all their native luxuriance. The train occupied forty minutes in fording the stream, when we halted for dinner on the western bank. A number of fishes were taken from the river during the dinner hour.

On Thursday the 12th we halted for dinner at a salt lake about two miles long and one mile wide.[27] Its waters were quite brackish, having a taste very much resembling that of Epsom salts. We were informed by our guide that there were salt springs a little to the north of this place from which considerable quantities of salt had been manufactured. The salt which we bought at Fort Garry for our journey was made somewhere between this place and Lake Winnipeg. We camped for the night at Shoal Lake, a beautiful body of crystalline water, being fed by springs, and abounding in fish. It is the source of a small stream which flows into the Assiniboine. On the 13th we passed through a fine country, pleasantly diversified by hills and valleys, wood and prairie lands; draped in a rich mantle of living green, thickly studded with little lakes, and gaily decked and enlivened by beds of flowers of almost unlimited variety and boundless extent. We dined this day on the Arrow River, a small swift stream twelve to fifteen feet wide, and camped for the night in the valley on the west side of the Birdtail River.[28] This is another branch of the Assiniboine, about thirty feet wide and three or four feet deep where we crossed it. It is one of the few streams in this section of the country that flow over rocky beds.

Crossing the Assiniboine from the East Side

At 10 o'clock in the forenoon of Saturday the 14th we reached the top of the hill overlooking the Assiniboine, at its confluence with the Qu'Appelle River and Beaver Creek. Here a most magnificent and picturesque view was presented to us. The bank upon which we stood was about three hundred feet high; directly opposite to us Beaver Creek could be seen emerging from between hills of equal altitude; away to the right, from between like precipitous banks, the waters of the Qu'Appelle were comingling with those of the "Stony River;"[29] Fort Ellice, a lone habitation, crowned the summit of the hill on the opposite side of the river; while at our feet the Assiniboine, dwindled away in the distance to the proportions of a rivulet, was winding its tortuous course through the valley below.[30] The descent to the river was very steep and rocky, but we managed to get down without more serious accident than the upsetting of a cart or two. Part of our company began crossing the river immediately upon our arrival; the rest set about preparing dinner. The crossing was effected by means of a scow which was drawn backward and forward by a rawhide rope stretched across the stream and made fast at both ends. The scow, although suitable enough for the purpose, was a rude affair, the property of the Hudson Bay Company, and was only large enough to carry a single ox and cart at a time; and as the current at the ferry was very strong, and, considering the great number of times the process had to be repeated, our crossing was a tedious and laborious operation. It was 4 o'clock by the time the last cart was over, when we ascended the hill by a rough and rugged road and camped at Fort Ellice.

We found the fort, which is situated upon Beaver Creek, about a mile and a half from its junction with the Assiniboine, in a rather dilapidated condition, but timber was just being prepared for the erection of new buildings on another site considerably nearer the Assiniboine.[31] Mr. McKay, the master of the fort,[32] is an obliging gentleman, and, in common with the rest of his countrymen, keeps a prudent eye to business, and a sharp lookout after the bawbees.[33] The 15th, being Sabbath, was spent in camp, the weather being cold with a driving rain from the south-east. The Rev. Mr. Settee, an Indian missionary of Fort Pelly, preached in Mr. McKay's house at 1 o'clock.[34] The rain still prevailing on Monday we remained at Ellice until after dinner, and employed the forenoon in making sundry repairs to carts, harness, &c., and in making such additional purchases for our outfit as two weeks travel and experience had shown to be necessary. From Fort Garry to this point our course was due west, and from Fort Ellice onward our general direction was north-west. We left Fort Ellice at 1 o'clock, P.M., and after driving a few miles reached the crossing of the Qu'Appelle.

In Difficulties

In descending the hill, which was very long and steep, several accidents occurred, one of which had well nigh proved fatal. The ox, belonging to Mr. Morrow, of Montreal, having become unmanageable, began running down the hill, dragging Mr. Morrow with him, and the road being very slippery with the rain, he fell under the cart and one of the wheels passed over his head.[35] When first picked up he was insensible, but Dr. Stevenson,[36] who was at hand, having dressed his wound, he soon recovered, and in a few days was able to take his place as before.

We crossed the Qu'Appelle in the same manner as the Assiniboine, but the river being narrow and the current slower, we were able to manage a scow large enough to carry two oxen and carts at a time, so that our transit occupied a much shorter time. For the use of these boats we paid to the agent of the Hudson Bay Company fifty cents for each animal and cart, amounting in all to a trifle over fifty dollars. After crossing we pursued our journey for a short distance up the Qu'Appelle, ascending the hill about two miles above the ferry, and camped for the night at a spring on the top of the bank. It never ceased raining during the whole afternoon, so that when we camped we were thoroughly drenched, and, as we had no opportunity for drying, we were compelled to lie down as we were in our wet clothes; this was the beginning of our experience in such exposures. On Tuesday the 17th we made a very long drive of thirty miles, over a good road and through a beautiful country, and camped for the night on the western side of Gulch Creek, a tributary of the

Caught in a Thunderstorm. Camping in a Hurry

Qu'Appelle.[37] The weather at this time was remarkably cold, and we were somewhat surprised upon rising on the morning of the 18th to find everything white with frost, and a covering of ice an eighth of an inch thick upon the water in our camp kettles. On account of the frost on the grass our animals did not appear to feed very well, and owing to the long drive yesterday we did not strike our tents until 6 o'clock.

When the train was ready to start this morning it was observed that our guide did not take his place at the head of the train as usual, and, upon making enquiries after him it was discovered that he had borrowed a gun from the late Mr. Patterson [Pattison] for the avowed purpose of hunting at a little distance from the trail, and that he had ridden southward. A change in his conduct towards the company, and an unusual reserve in his intercourse with us had been remembered for a day or two, but we were completely in his power, and in order to retain his confidence it was necessary that we should cultivate a confidence in him, and never betray the slightest distrust in his faithfulness. He was therefore allowed to go as he pleased, without any restraint; yet we were not altogether free from apprehensions respecting his intentions. The day wore on, the dinner hour passed, camping time came, and still no guide; but it was not until after supper, when the company were assembled within the corral to deliberate upon our situation, that we could be brought to believe that we had really been the victims of treachery. Now our worst fears were realized; our guide had deserted us. The heartless villain who could perpetrate such a crime deserves the universal execration of mankind; and we feel it to be a bounden duty now to pass around the name of Charles Rochette that stern retributive justice may yet overtake him. Some grave charges were also laid against Bishop Taché for an alleged complicity with Rochette, for the purpose of obtaining the money; that charity, however, "which thinketh no evil," and a regard for the sanctity of his office, compel us to acquit that gentleman of any connection with, or knowledge of, so monstrous a transaction.

After the guide had gone it was considered prudent to increase our vigilance, lest he or some of his accomplices might be prowling about, watching for an opportunity to steal our animals. We were now thrown entirely upon our own resources, but we had obtained such a knowledge of the country, and of the marks by which the trails across the plains were distinguished, as enabled us to find our way without any very serious difficulty.

The country passed through between the 18th and 24th, was of a very monotonous character, consisting almost entirely of open plains, destitute of timber and living streams, but containing a great many little lakes, the majority of which were of a strongly mineral or alkaline nature. These lakes were literally alive with ducks, but, as it was their breeding season, we shot very few of them. The road, too, for this distance, was uniformly good, with the exception of an occasional slough in the vicinity of these little lakes, some of which we had to fill with brush before we could drive over them. At 9 o'clock on the morning of the 24th, we passed a deserted trading post of the Hudson Bay Company, situated among the Touchwood Hills,[38] and at 4 o'clock in the afternoon of the same day we left the Hills, and descended again into the plains. Some of these hills are elevated to a considerable height above the surrounding plains, and contain some lovely spots, which it seemed a pity should have remained so long waste and desolate. We gathered to-

Prairie Treeless

day the first ripe strawberries of the season. On the 25th we passed an immense, trackless prairie, so absolutely destitute of anything in the shape of a tree that it was impossible to procure a single stick for cooking our food. We were in the habit, however, whenever the country ahead of us appeared to be without wood, of gathering a little which we carried along with us on our carts. On Thursday the 26th we travelled through a magnificent country of alternate woods and prairies, bearing a most luxuriant growth of grass, and traversed in all directions by old buffalo trails. It had evidently at some time been the resort and pasture-land of immense herds of these animals, as their bones were thickly scattered over the whole country. The weather now was exceedingly hot, and the mosquitoes at times appeared in such myriads as almost to darken the air. We found them very troublesome both to our animals and ourselves, the more sensitive of us being almost driven to distraction by their incessant attacks. At 10 o'clock, A.M., of the 27th, about sixty miles west of the Thickwood Hills, we passed three old deserted houses, but we could not find out when, or by whom, they were built, or for what purpose they were used, most likely by some trappers or hunters at a time when game was more plentiful in these regions. We experienced considerable difficulty this afternoon in finding a camping ground, as nearly all the water was either salt or alkaline, and having driven until 9 o'clock, three hours later than our usual time, we pitched our tents by the side of a small lake, the waters of which were strongly sulphurious.

We had now succeeded in establishing such order and discipline in the company, and all our movements were executed with such military precision, that, within fifteen minutes after the order to start was given, and the word, "Every man to his ox," had been passed round the camp, all the animals would be brought in and harnessed, the tents and baggage packed up and loaded, and the whole train would be in motion. On Saturday, the 28th, we came upon an immense valley, enclosed by high hills along which we travelled nearly all day,[39] and camped for the night at another alkali lake.

The fatigues of the journey were now beginning to have an injurious effect upon our animals, as well as upon the tempers and dispositions of the men, and especially towards the end of the week were these effects more apparent, when frequent disagreements and petty disputes or quarrels of a more serious kind would take place, when each was ready to contradict the other, and at the slightest occasion, or without any occasion, to take offence. But to-morrow would be the Sabbath; and no wonder that its approach should be regarded with pleasurable anticipations, as furnishing an opportunity for restoring the exhausted energies of both man and beast, for smoothing down the asperities of our natures, and, by allowing us time for reflection, for regaining a just appreciation of our duties toward one another; and the vigor with which our journey would be prosecuted, and the cordiality and good-feeling that characterized our intercourse after our accustomed rest on the first day of the week, are sufficient evidence to us that the law of the Sabbath is of physical, as well as of moral obligation, and that its precepts cannot be violated with impunity. We certainly have had much reason gratefully to adore that infinite wisdom and goodness that provided for us such a rest.

Over the Camp Fire

At 7 o'clock in the morning of Monday the last day of June we reached the South Branch of the Great Saskatchewan River. We found it a noble stream, about three hundred yards wide with a moderately strong current, and flowing between lofty banks;[40] but its waters, like those of the Red River, Assiniboine and Qu'Appelle, are quite muddy, owing to the nature of the soil through which they flow. Here we found a bateau or York boat, belonging to the Hudson Bay Company, with which we conveyed our stuff over. This boat was on the opposite or north side of the river when we came up, and the late lamented Capt. Robertson of the Goderich party, and Mr. Cogswell of Detroit swam across and brought it back. We then unharnessed our animals, and, having unloaded the carts and taken off the wheels, piled them into the boat, carrying about six carts with their loads at a time. An occurrence happened here which for the moment cast a gloom over the whole company. We had to swim our animals across the river, and in driving into the stream some of those that were unwilling to swim, Mr. Robert Kelso, of the Acton party, went beyond his depth, and but for the timely arrival and assistance of Messrs. Strachan and Reid, two expert swimmers, he must have found a watery grave.[41] When taken out of the water he was to all appearance beyond hope, but the usual remedies having been applied he was in time restored to consciousness.[42] The crossing occupied nearly the whole day, and it was 5 o'clock, P.M., by the time the last boat load was discharged.

We camped for the night in the valley of the Saskatchewan, about one mile from the river. At 11 o'clock, A.M. on Tuesday, the 1st day of July, we reached the North Branch of the Saskatchewan, at the Carleton House.[43] The valley, where we crossed it from the South to the North Branch, is about 18 miles wide. We found the North Branch in all respects very much like the South, only a little smaller. At the Carleton House we purchased some fresh buffalo meat that had just been brought in by the hunters; it resembles beef, but is a little coarser in the grain, and more juicy. We relished it very much. Our crossing here was effected in the same manner as at the South Branch; it employed us until after dark, and was accomplished in safety. For the use of the boat here we paid 12½ cents per cart. The country between this point and Fort Pitt was of a somewhat different character from what we had passed hitherto, being more broken and hilly, with more running streams and fewer ponds of stagnant water. The weather, particularly at night, was much cooler than the same season would be found in Canada, with occasional showers of rain, but upon the whole remarkably pleasant. Nothing of special importance occurred on this part of the journey. We passed the Thickwood Hills on the 3d, and the Lumpy Hills on the 4th.[44] On this day also we passed through some immense fields of splendid strawberries, and at supper we treated ourselves to a huge dish of strawberries and cream. Large numbers of wolves were now continually prowling about us—they were very attentive to our company, forming our rear guard while on the march during the day, and entertaining us at night with repeated concerts.[45]

At 9 o'clock on Wednesday morning, the 9th of July, we reached Fort Pitt.[46] This is another Hudson Bay station, and is situated on the north side of the North Saskatchewan, nearly midway between the Carleton House and Edmonton. Between Fort Pitt and Edmonton there are two trails, one on each side of the river; but neither of them is very plain as the Hudson Bay Company travel between these points chiefly with boats. We had not experienced much difficulty in following the trail since we were deserted by our first guide, but the gentleman in charge of Fort Pitt advised us not to attempt the remainder of the road without a guide, and recommended one Mitchelle [Michel], an Iroquois Indian, to serve in that capacity.[47] He also advised us to take the trail on the south side of the river, as it was better and shorter than that upon the north side. We found Mitchelle a faithful and intelligent guide, and were convinced of the wisdom of the course we had adopted before reaching Edmonton, as the trail was so indistinct that it would have been impossible to have found it without a guide. We therefore re-crossed to the south side, our transit being safely accomplished in the same manner as our previous crossing, and camped on the bank where we remained until Thursday morning, when we resumed our journey. An exciting chase after a pair of fawns took place on Thursday afternoon, and served to relieve the monotony of our march although no one was fortunate enough to capture the animals. On Friday morning Mr. John Fannin shot a very large wolf, that had ventured too near to our camp.

Bridge Breaking Down

Hitherto the weather had been singularly favorable for our purpose; we had not been delayed a single day on account of rain, and altogether our journey had been tolerably comfortable; but now we were to have a change in the programme. At half-past 4 o'clock this afternoon it began raining heavily, and continued, with but little intermission, during the whole succeeding eleven days. We camped for the night at 5 o'clock, after being thoroughly wet, and remained there until Monday morning, the 14th, the rain pouring the whole time. At this time, the weather having cleared up for a little, we struck our tents and pushed forward, as we were desirous of making the best possible use of our time, but had not proceeded very far when we were compelled to halt again, as the rain was coming down in torrents and wetting everything in our carts. And thus we plodded along, at one time driving on regardless of the rain, and at another time camping in a vain attempt to keep ourselves and our provisions dry. But a new difficulty now presented itself. The country through which we were now passing was traversed and intersected by innumerable streams, tributaries of the Saskatchewan, and these had become so much swollen by the extraordinary floods as to render fording impossible. The only way we could get over was by bridging, and to such an extent had the water risen that between the 18th and 21st we built *eight bridges,*[48] averaging from forty to one hundred feet in length, besides wading without much ceremony through everything not more than *four feet* in depth. Upon one occasion, when the water from one of these streams was spread to a great distance over the adjoining plain, and after we had waded for at least half a mile up to our waists, it became a question with some of the company whether it was really the Overland

Rather Deep

Route, that we were travelling, but all doubt upon the subject was at once removed by an assurance from Mr. Fannin that it was at least *three feet Overland* where he had tried it.

On Monday, the 21st day of July, at half-past 7 o'clock in the afternoon, we reached the crossing of the Saskatchewan at a point directly opposite to the Edmonton House, the sight of which was the signal for a hearty and tumultuous cheer, which was repeated again and again as the different parties came up, until the surrounding forests re-echoed with the sound.[49] During the preceeding eleven days our clothing had never been dry, we had just passed through what we considered a pretty tough time, and the toil-worn, jaded, forlorn and tattered appearance of the company was in striking and amusing contrast with our appearance a few months before; so marked, indeed, was the change that our most intimate friends at home could scarcely have recognized us. But our courage was still unbroken, and, although we had been much longer on the road than we anticipated, we had yet full confidence in our ability to reach the El Dorado of our hopes. All the boats at this point belonging to the Hudson Bay Company had been carried away by the unusual floods a few days before our arrival, so that we had no facilities for crossing, and we were compelled to remain in camp, on the opposite side of the river, until Thursday, the 25th, when those who had been sent down the river after the boats returned with them.[50] We then crossed the Saskatchewan for the fourth time, in the same manner as we had previously done, all getting over safely.

We had often heard and read of the beauty and fertility of the Great Saskatchewan Valley; but after travelling through it for nearly a month we were satisfied that all description had failed to convey to the mind a full and accurate idea of its vast extent, the exuberance of its vegetation, the surpassing beauty of some of its parts, or its fitness and capacity for becoming the homes of a dense population; that, in short, the country must be seen to be appreciated. The Hudson Bay Company cultivate a small portion of land at each of their stations, and from the ample returns they obtain for their labor, and the value set upon flour by the people about the forts, as evinced by the eagerness with which they bought that article from our company, paying any price we might set upon it, it was a matter of surprise to us that more attention was not paid to agriculture, and particularly to the cultivation of wheat. Sufficient, however, was grown to give us an idea of the productiveness of the soil. From Mr. Brazeau, the gentleman in charge of the Edmonton House during the absence of Mr. Christie, the master,[51] *we learned that from a field of ten acres they reaped four hundred bushels,* or forty bushels to the acre, of prime wheat, equal to an average sample of Canadian wheat, and, what is more extraordinary, that wheat had been grown in the same field year after year in succession, for a period of about *thirty years,* and that, too, without the application of a particle of manure. The field was under the same crop again this year; it was just headed out when we were there, and promised a fair yield, although it was considerably injured by the drought that prevailed here in the early part of the season, as well as by the recent floods. We observed a field of barley, also, that had just headed out; it looked tolerably fair, having suffered somewhat from the same causes that affected the wheat. They consider about fifty bushels per acre an average yield. Potatoes, as well as other root-crops, grow most luxuriantly; the vines were in full blossom at the time of our visit. From a field containing about five or six acres they dug last year sixteen hundred bushels of potatoes. The rot is unknown.

We had an opportunity here of examining one of the natural resources of this region that will no doubt some day prove of incalculable value to the whole of this region. I refer to the vast beds of coal which crop out in the banks of the Saskatchewan at Edmonton, and extend for several hundred miles in a north-western direction. It appears in the face of the bank in several parallel beds or layers, varying from two to six feet in thickness, and interstratified with a kind of red clay that has the appearance of having been burnt. It is very easily obtained, lying, as it does, upon the surface. Another of the probable resources of this country, and which may yet be a chief agent in attracting hither a large population, is gold. That the precious metal does exist in *nearly all the streams* flowing through the Hudson Bay Territory, east of the Rocky Mountains, is beyond all question, since we seldom failed to raise the color wherever we prospected; but that it may be found in paying quantities is yet somewhat problematical.

Edmonton and Saskatchewan River

We were, however, assured by several parties living at Edmonton that large nuggets were frequently seen with the Indians, and that at low water the sand in the channel of the Saskatchewan literally glittered in the sun-light; and a person whom we met at Prairie Portage, who had acted for several years as interpreter to the Rev. Mr. Woolsey, Wesleyan Missionary at Edmonton,[52] and upon whom we could place considerable reliance, even went so far as to offer, for a consideration, to take us to diggings within five days walk of the Edmonton House, if he should return before we left the place, which he would guarantee to yield at least *fifteen dollars* a day to the hand, with rockers, and he would give us an opportunity to test their richness before he would expect his pay. Unfortunately he did not return to Edmonton before we left, so that we did not get an opportunity to take advantage of his offer as it was our intention to have done. It is not worth while, however, at this time, to indulge in conjecture or useless speculation upon this subject, neither is it pertinent to our present purpose that we should hazard a decided opinion respecting it, inasmuch as about twenty-five intelligent and determined fellows of our company remained at Edmonton for the purpose of exploring the country and prospecting the rivers nearer the mountains.[53] They were furnished with an ample supply of provisions, and we may look forward with deep interest for a report of their doings, as it will be likely to contain some definite and conclusive information upon this question that may be of vital importance not only to this territory but to British America.

We had now reached the destination for which we set out from Fort Garry, and in the mean time, the end of our journey; and it remained for us now to determine by what route we should next proceed and what pass we should take across the mountains. In the solution of this question we had frequent interviews with Mr. Brazeau, of Edmonton, the Rev. Mr. Woolsey, who had been several years in the country; Thomas Clover,[54] Timolean Love's companion; Mr. Alexander, a clerk in the Hudson Bay Company who had recently returned from the Jasper House; besides a number of Freemen whose names I did not learn, many of whom were born and brought up in the neighborhood of the mountains. All parties with whom we conversed on the subject, both at this time and previously, agreed that the Boundary, Cootanie [Kootenay] and Sinclair Passes were the easiest and presented the fewest difficulties; but recommended the Leather, Cow-dung Lake, or Jasper Pass [all names for what is now called Yellowhead Pass] for our purpose, as being the shortest and most direct way to Cariboo; altho' some of them represented the road as nearly impassable, and foresaw difficulties and dangers which they considered almost insurmountable.[55] After thoroughly examining the matter, and carefully comparing notes, we decided to try the Leather Pass. Our next care was to secure another guide who could lead us safely over the mountains, to the head waters of the Fraser. This we found in the person of one André Cardinal, a Freeman of St. Albert, who was born at the Jasper House, where he spent the greater portion of his life;[56] who had passed over the road between his birthplace and Edmonton *twenty-nine times,* and several times between Jasper and Tête Jaune Cache,[57] at the head of the Fraser, and for whose services we paid fifty dollars in cash, an ox and cart, 1 cwt. of flour and a few groceries. We had been busily employed in the mean time exchanging our oxen and carts for horses and pack-saddles, and in disposing of such articles as we found too bulky for packing. As we were still at Edmonton on Sabbath, July 27th, we had the pleasure of listening to a sermon by the Rev. Mr. Woolsey at 11 o'clock in the fort, and at 4 o'clock in our own camp.

On the Prairies near Edmonton

As none of us were accustomed to packing, our preparations here occupied a considerable time, so that we were not ready to leave till Tuesday morning, July 29th, having remained at Edmonton a whole week. At 9 o'clock, A.M. of this day we started again, our party being now reduced to 125, with about 140 animals, having purchased a number of additional horses here. Our animals were loaded with from 150 to 250 lbs. each. We reached the settlement of St. Albert, at Big Lake, 10 miles from Edmonton, at 1 o'clock, and remained there all night.[58] Settlements

were first made here about two or three years ago, and contain now about
twenty families, consisting chiefly of Freemen, persons who have
fulfilled their term of service with the Hudson Bay Company, and
received their discharges. It is a very fertile spot, beautifully situated on
the eastern side of Big Lake, which furnishes a plentiful supply of fish,
and, what is an important desideratum in this, as in all prairie countries,
there is an abundance of timber suitable for building and other purposes
in its immediate vicinity. Upon the farm and in the gardens attached to
the Catholic Mission at St. Albert we observed a great variety of crops,
including wheat, barley, oats, peas, buckwheat, Indian-corn, potatoes,
turnips, beets, carrots, cabbages, onions, radishes, &c., all of which
looked well and some of them promised a most abundant crop.
Notwithstanding the great disadvantage at which we saw this part of the
country, on account of the heavy rains and the consequent super-
abundance of water everywhere, we could not help admiring the general
fertility.

Two short days drive from this point brought us to St. Ann's Lake
[Lac Ste Anne], on the shore of which we camped on Thursday night,[59]
having passed over an exceedingly rough road, built one bridge and
endured a drizzling rain the greater part of the time. On Friday morning,
August 1st, we drove about two miles to St. Ann's settlement, or village,
where we again halted. Here we found a trading post of the Hudson Bay
Company, and a considerable settlement.[60] It is 50 miles from Edmonton. A few years ago it is said to have contained some fifty families, but a
part of them have lately removed to St. Albert, the settlement above
described. Here we were fortunate enough to obtain some splendid new
potatoes, which, with other vegetables, appear to grow almost spon-
taneously, and which, for size and quality, I have never seen excelled at
this season in any country. The immense quantities and numberless
varieties of berries produced here, including rasp, dew, straw and
gooseberries, red and black currants, &c., are almost incredible, and the
most careful cultivation at home has failed to produce anything, so far as
I have seen, that could nearly equal the samples of black currants we saw
growing wild. The lake of St. Ann's is a beautiful body of water, about 10
miles long and 4 miles wide, and abounds in whitefish. On Saturday, the
2nd day of August, we left St. Ann's, having abandoned our last cart
there.[61]

Our way for the remainder of our journey was totally different from
what we had before passed through; for, instead of the hard and level
roads with which we had been favored in the first part of our journey,
swamps and hills and streams alternated, and dense forests, where we
were obliged to keep a gang of men ahead of the train to chop out the
brush and fallen timber, were substituted for open prairies. We halted
this day for dinner on the bank of Sturgeon River, and camped for the

St. Anns, R.C.

night by the Lake of Many Hills [Lake Isle], where we remained until Monday morning, the 4th of August.[62] While we remained here, Mr. W. Sellars [Sellar], of Huntingdon, who had waited at Edmonton for the arrival of Dr. Symington's party, overtook us, bringing up letters from Fort Garry for some of our number, and a copy of the Toronto *Globe* of the 16th of May, which was the last intelligence we received from the outside world until we reached the end of our journey.

At 4 o'clock in the afternoon of this day we camped on the bank of the Pembina River. The first object of interest that claimed our attention upon our arrival here was the coal, which again crops out, in the banks of this stream, as at Edmonton. It appears here in a single stratum of perfectly pure coal, and where it is visible above water, about twelve feet in thickness. At our crossing place it formed the bed of the river, upon which we walked in fording, and had a considerable inclination toward the surface of the ground as you descend the stream. In the evening bright coal fires were blazing in every part of our camp, and those who were judges pronounced it a superior article. Shortly after camping our notice was attracted by a heavy cloud of smoke which hung along the brow of a hill at a short distance to the left of the trail by which we came down. We immediately ascended the hill to ascertain, if possible, whence the smoke proceeded, and upon reaching the summit we found, to our astonishment, that it was issuing from the top of the hill; that we were actually standing upon a volcano, and that beneath our feet still lay some of the smouldering embers of those mighty subterranean fires that at some remote period of time had caused those terrible convulsions in the crust of the earth that are so apparent throughout a great portion of this region.[63] The crater appeared to be choked up by the loose soil on the surface continuously crumbling down into it, so that the smoke instead of escaping by a single aperture seemed to permeate the whole top of the mound. The earth on the surface is quite hot, destroying all signs of vegetation for some distance around, and when turned up with a spade we were unable to bear our hands upon it. There was a strong smell as of escaping gas perceptible in its neighborhood.

Crossing Pembina River

The weather on the morning of the 5th was very clear, and so cold that the dew, which fell very copiously, froze, and hung in small icicles from the leaves. Our crossing here, which occupied the whole of Tuesday forenoon, was one of the busiest and most exciting scenes of our trip, and would have furnished a splendid subject for "our special artist." Part of our goods were carried over in boats made by spreading out our tents and placing our baggage in the centre, and then drawing up the edges with a lariat; another line was then made fast to this, by which two men on horseback towed it across, while two others waded into the water, holding on to the float behind to keep it from upsetting. Another portion of them was carried on horseback, a man mounting the horse and taking the stuff up before him, where, as the water was just up to the horses' backs, he could have a chance to hold it up if it were likely to get wet; and the balance, that could not be injured by being wet, was carried over without unpacking. On the eastern side of the river a number of men might be seen dispatching our goods by these different modes of conveyance, and as many more on the opposite side busily engaged in receiving and re-arranging them in packs, while the river was full of animals going and returning, loaded or empty; here were a couple tugging away against the current with their canvas boat, while the luckless wights, up to their necks in the water, held on behind; there a bewildered equestrian was making a vain attempt to guide his steed across the stream, while his nervous friend, to whom he had given a deck passage, held him firmly in his arms, and put forth many well directed efforts to repay his generosity by ducking them both; and yonder, another bold navigator astride of an ox, sometimes in the water and sometimes out, was boxing the compass in his ineffectual endeavors to persuade his boon companion to shape his course toward sundown. All having got safely over we left the Pembina River after dinner, and camped for the night on Buffalo-dung [Lobstick] River, a tributary of the Pembina.[64] We forded this river soon after starting on the following morning, where the water was about three feet deep.

Horse Bogged

During the forenoon of Friday the 8th we passed over a portion of the road that language is absolutely inadequate to describe. To say that it was horrible expresses but half the truth.[65] It consisted of an interminable swamp, in which nearly the whole train would be mired at once, and over which we carried a considerable portion of our packs on our shoulders. We halted for dinner on Root River [Carrot Creek], a branch of McLeod's, having passed at 11 o'clock the point from which, on a clear day, the first view of the Rocky Mountains can be obtained. The weather to-day was too hazy. On Saturday the 9th, we made a long drive through a dense forest, consisting chiefly of spruce, pine and poplar, in the middle of which we came upon a solitary grave. From a rude inscription upon the trunk of a tree hard by, we learned that it contained the last remains of one James Mokerty, who died while passing through these wilds in October, 1860. At half-past 4 o'clock this afternoon we reached the crossing of McLeod's River, when we forded it without removing our packs, and camped upon the west bank immediately after. McLeod's River is a considerable stream, about one hundred and fifty yards wide, and a branch of the Athabaska. We had some difficulty in fording this stream, as the current was very strong and the water exceedingly cold, and Messrs. Willox and Gilbert narrowly escaped drowning by being swept off by the current into deep water.[66] Here we remained till Monday morning the 11th. Our trail, which was an extremely rough one, lay for the following three days along the northern bank of McLeod's River, and during this time we forded a great many rapid streams.

On Wednesday, the 13th, precisely at 12 o'clock, noon, as the train emerged from a thick spruce swamp and halted for dinner upon a slight eminence, we obtained the first distinct view of the Rocky Mountains.[67] Although we were yet about one hundred miles from them, their dark outline was plainly visible far above the level of the horizon, and their lofty snow-clad peaks, standing out in bold relief against the blue sky beyond, and glistening in the sunlight, gave them the appearance of fleecy clouds floating in the distance. The company were enraptured at the sight of them; for whatever dangers or difficulties might possibly be in store for us among them, all were heartily tired of the endless succession of hills and streams and swamps, and swamps and streams and hills, and were willing to face almost any danger that would be likely to terminate or vary our toils.

On Thursday our guide had to hunt up an entirely new trail, as the unusual rush of water this year had in many places quite changed the position of the river, and completely washed away all traces of the old trail. After a long, weary drive on Friday, the 15th, we camped for the night on the bank of the Athabaska. This is a beautiful stream of clear, cold water, which takes its rise in the mountains, and is fed by springs and melting snow. Here we met some half-breeds who were on their way from the Jasper House to Edmonton, and from whom we purchased a piece of a mountain sheep which they had recently killed. We travelled for four days succeeding this time along the south bank of the Athabaska, a part of the time over a very good road. We camped on Saturday night, the 16th, on Prairie River[68] [Maskuta Creek], a tributary of the Athabaska, in full view of the mountains, where we remained until Monday morning. One day's drive from this point brought us to the mountains, at the foot of which we camped on Monday night.

If it be true, as has been said, that "wherever there is vastness, there dwells sublimity," we were presented with a view at once sublimely grand and overpowering. On our left, and immediately overlooking our camping ground, a stupendous pile of rocks rose perpendicularly to the height of about one thousand feet; across the Athabaska, and directly opposite to this, Mount Lacomb reared its rocky head to a still greater elevation, and behind us, Mount Mayette [Miette], with its cold and craggy cliffs crowned with eternal snows, towered proudly far above the whole.[69] Two of our company ascended the rock on the left of our camp, and when they reached the top they were scarcely discernible; they appeared like pigmies, and their loudest shout was scarcely audible to the rest of us at the bottom.

In examining and comparing these apparently confused and disordered heaps on opposite sides of the river, one cannot help remarking the striking similarity in many particulars that exists between them. In the order of their strata, their size or thickness, their dip or inclination, their composition, and indeed their whole geological structure, there is such a correspondence as must convince the most casual observer that at some period in the world's history they formed contiguous and adjacent portions of the crust of the earth; while the present disrupted condition of these huge masses of rock, and the violent contortions to which they have evidently been subjected, will convey to the mind some faint idea of the irresistible power of those internal fires, that mighty agency by which these terrible convulsions have been effected. And from a consideration of these terrestrial objects, the meditative mind, by a natural and easy gradation, will rise to the contemplation of that almighty and infinite Being, who makes all these powers subservient to His will, who spoke a world into existence,—at whose sovereign fiat a universe was created.

During the night of the 18th we were visited with a thunder storm, the effect of which was greatly heightened by our close proximity to the scene of the elementary conflict, and the recollection of which shall never be effaced from my memory. A heavy black cloud, that appeared to hang below the mountain tops, slowly floated across our zenith, completely shutting out the heavens and enveloping us in impenetrable darkness. Presently all the surrounding objects were highly illuminated for an instant, while the liquid fire coursed along the cloud, or darted from peak to peak, to be succeeded the next moment by a still deeper gloom, and followed immediately by deafening peals of thunder, which were re-echoed again and again from all sides of our amphitheatre, producing such a scene of terrific grandeur as I shall not attempt to describe.

On Tuesday the 19th we passed one of the most dangerous portions of our road. Our trail lay over a pretty high mountain, and near the top consisted of a very narrow pathway, with a perpendicular wall of rocks on one side, and a steep declivity down to the edge of a precipice several hundred feet high on the other. Here a single blunder, one false step for either man or beast, and no human power could save him from instant destruction.[70] The whole train passed it in safety. When we were on the top of this mountain we could see the Jasper House, a perfect picture of loneliness and solitude, away below us in the valley on the opposite, or north side of the Athabasca River, where from our elevation it appeared no larger than a hen-coop.[71] This is another Station of the Hudson Bay Company, which some of their agents visit annually, at a certain season, for the purpose of trading with the Shoushwaps and other Indians of the Rocky Mountains. It was shut up at this time.

We halted for dinner this day on the shore of White-fish Lake [Talbot Lake], being surrounded by Russian Jack, the Black Mountain and Smith's Peak,[72] and camped for night on a flat near the Athabaska after having climbed two or three very rugged mountains. At 8 o'clock in the morning of the 20th we reached the crossing place of the Athabaska River. We immediately set about building rafts, with which we floated ourselves and goods over, swimming our animals. We took dinner on the northern bank of the river after all were safely over. The river here is about one hundred yards wide and fifteen to twenty feet deep, with a strong current. Here we found prospects which, according to the judgment of some Californian miners who accompanied us, would yield from three to four dollars a day.[73] These were the most encouraging returns we met with, although it is quite possible we may have passed near by, or even over, rich diggings, since our prospecting was confined merely to washing a pan or two of sand, taken from the surface along the edges of the streams at whatever point our road might chance to cross them, without looking for any more promising localities; entrusting the important duty of making a more thorough examination to those of our number who remained behind us.

At 8 o'clock on Thursday morning the 21st, we passed the ruins of Henry's House, a deserted trading post of the Hudson Bay Company.[74] It is situated on the north side of the Athabaska, near its confluence with the Mayette. Shortly after this we reached the Mayette River, which we followed until we struck the head waters of the Fraser. Our progress along this stream was rather slow, both on account of the great quantity of fallen timber that obstructed our path, and the number of times we had to ford the stream. It is a mountain torrent that rushes down a rocky

Through the Woods and Bugs

gorge, and our trail lay for a short distance on one side, and then on the other, so that in the short space of two hours we waded through it no less than seven times, while the water threatened to sweep us off our feet, and "Oh! how cold." During the forenoon of the 22nd we crossed the Mayette twice, and camped for the night on the shore of Cow-dung Lake [Yellowhead Lake].[75]

At 4 o'clock this afternoon we passed the heights of land or dividing ridge between the waters which flow to the east and those which flow to the west of the Rocky Mountains. We were somewhat surprised to find the weather in the valleys of this elevated region so mild and warm, surrounded as they were on every side with immense heaps of perpetual snow, while some of the vast glaciers extended far down toward them. There was a clearness, a lightness and salubrity about the atmosphere that was really delightful. Shortly after we passed the dividing ridge we struck the mighty Fraser at a point where we crossed it at a single step.

During the first part of our journey we found such rich and abundant pasturage for our animals that some of our oxen, that left Fort Garry in very ordinary condition, were fit for beef by the time we reached Edmonton; but ever since we left the Saskatchewan the feed had been gradually failing, and for several days past there had been but very little for them to eat, so that they were rapidly giving out, and two or three were abandoned nearly every day, being unable to travel any further. When we started from the Selkirk Settlement we expected to reach the end of our journey in about two months, and provided ourselves with what we considered a plentiful supply of provisions—168 lbs. of flour and 50 lbs. of pemican, besides a variety of other articles to each man; but we had been nearly three months already on the way, and were yet in the middle of the mountains without any certain knowledge of what was before us, and our stock of provisions was running so low that, as a precautionary measure, we had been for some time upon short allowance. Here we ate our last pemican, when we found it necessary to kill an ox. Our supply of salt was nearly exhausted, and we had to cure our meat by cutting it into thin strips and drying it over the fire.

On Saturday the 23d our guide intended to camp for the night on Moose Lake, but owing to the desperate condition of the roads we were unable to reach it; we camped upon the Fraser within about four miles of it, where the feed was very scarce. We were compelled to move from this spot on Sabbath the 24th in order to obtain pasturage for our animals, and camped again at the western end of Moose Lake. Feed still very indifferent. We dined this day upon a dish so delicate and rare that it might have tempted the palate of Epicurus himself; so nice, indeed, was it, that I have some little hesitation in naming it, lest we might be censured for living too luxuriously by the way. It was a *roasted skunk,* which our guide prepared and served up to us in true Indian style.[76] After we had finished our repast, which all appeared to relish, we wondered that we had not discovered its good qualities sooner, and unanimously resolved, that his skunkship had been a slandered and much abused individual. Although it is not my province at this time to moralize, yet I cannot help remarking that this incident may serve to remind us how often we allow our prejudices to deprive us of the enjoyment of substantial good; and that we are creatures of comparison, and governed in a great measure by external circumstances, knowing nothing of absolute good or positive pleasure but by a comparison with its converse, and relishing under certain conditions what we would nauseate under others. Our trail this day followed along the shore of Moose Lake, which is nine miles long. The weather [was] still remarkably fine.

On Monday the 25th we drove for two hours and fifteen minutes when we came upon a beautiful valley, bearing the most luxuriant crop of grass we had seen for many a day, where we halted to feed our hungry animals, and took dinner, treating ourselves to-day to a piece of porcupine, which was also esteemed a great delicacy. During the day we found vast quantities of huckleberries of extraordinary size. We camped this night in the woods on the side of a mountain, where there was not a mouthful of feed for our animals excepting what they browsed from the trees. The long drives we were compelled to make over such a road without sufficient feed now told fearfully upon the poor beasts, which were failing rapidly, and it was fortunate that we were nearly over, as it was evident they could not endure such treatment much longer. We noticed a considerable change in the character of the timber since we began to descend the mountains; for while that upon the eastern slope consisted exclusively of spruce, pine, poplar and small willows, upon the western side we met cedar, hemlock, balsam and soft maple, in addition. The Fraser had now become a large stream, and was contin- ually receiving fresh additions from numberless tributaries, which we met at every little interval rushing down the declivities of the mountains with fearful impetuosity.

About mid-day on the 26th we passed a dangerous spot, very much like that opposite to the Jasper House on the Athabaska. We did not venture our horses across it loaded, but unpacked them and carried our provisions over on our shoulders. During the afternoon we crossed a great many streams of intensely cold water, and camped for night in a kind of amphitheatre surrounded on all sides with lofty snow-capped peaks. We were early roused from our slumbers on Wednesday morning by our guide shouting through the camp, "Hurrah! for Tête Jaune Cache," and were informed that we should reach the Cache, if no misfortune befel us, some time during the day; an announcement that was received by the company with unaffected enthusiasm.

Accordingly, at 4 o'clock in the afternoon of this day, we were delighted with a view of the welcome and long-looked-for spot. We had now completed the second stage of our journey; and it only remained for us to undertake the third and last. By the time we reached the Cache, our stock of provisions was nearly exhausted, some parties being entirely out of flour, and living solely upon beef without salt. We were very glad, therefore, to find a camp of Shoushwap Indians here, from whom we got some dried salmon and berry cakes in exchange for amunition, shirts, handkerchiefs, needles, thread or any article almost we might choose to part with. The cakes were made of huckle and june or service berries, which grow here in very great abundance, by bruising the berries to a pulp and then spreading them out upon thin sticks to dry.

A fine plain extends to some distance on the south side of the Fraser at this point, producing some fine pasturage, and an open valley which we found on the north side furnished an abundance of feed for all our animals while we remained at the Cache. The weather during our stay here was remarkably pleasant.

Up to this point we had either been accompanied by a guide, or had such information respecting our way, that we could proceed with safety, but regarding the concluding portion of our journey it was all doubt and uncertainty. In our agreement with André Cardinal, our guide, it was stipulated that if he could find a Shoushwap here, who was acquainted with the trail into Cariboo, he was to hire him as a guide, and that Cardinal himself would accompany us as interpreter. But the Indians whom we met here knew nothing of any trail in that direction, nor even of the place we wished to reach. They were in the habit of hunting in the direction of the Columbia and Thompson Rivers, and fishing for a short distance down the Fraser, which they represented as very dangerous, a representation which, unfortunately, we found to be too true. We were therefore left to rely upon our own judgment as to the best way to proceed, or to depend merely upon blind chance. After fully considering our situation, and the probable difficulties that might be in our way, we decided to build rafts and canoes and float down the Fraser, taking a few animals with us as a security against starvation, and to send the remainder of our horses across the country southward, toward the head waters of the Thompson, in the hands of a few of the company who volunteered for that purpose. Messrs. A. Thompson, Fannin, Putnam and Fortune volunteered from the Queenston party, there being about twenty in all.[77] In pursuance of this determination we built a number of rafts, about 40 feet long, and 18 feet wide; and several canoes, some of which were lashed together in pairs to prevent them from upsetting. Besides these we procured some others from the Indians, in exchange for horses. As we were rather short of axes, and other tools, our preparations here occupied considerable time, so that we were detained until Monday, the 1st day of September. At 3 o'clock P.M. of this day, after taking leave of our companions, whom we had but little hopes of meeting again, and in regard to some of whom our worst fears have been realized, we committed ourselves to the mercy of the Fraser, amid the sorrowful exclamations of the Indians, "Poor white men no more."[78]

The raft which carried the Queenston party was put in charge of Mr. Robt. Harkness. The river for some distance below the Cache is very crooked, and in some places pretty narrow, and the current being very swift, we had some difficulty in keeping the raft off the rocks. The mountains along this part of the stream are very rugged, and approach close to the river on both sides, leaving but a very narrow channel through which the waters wind their way, following a peculiarly serpentine course around the bases of the hills. We estimated the current to be about five miles an hour. The weather during the whole time that we were upon the Fraser, until we reached Fort George, was very wet, cold and uncomfortable. We usually floated as long as we could find the channel, cooking our meals on the raft, and running from daylight till dark.

On Tuesday afternoon, when, according to our reckoning, we had made 70 miles from the Cache, we came upon a portion of the river which flows through an exceedingly level country; and where the sluggish stream, widening out the the distance of fully a mile, does not run at a faster rate than two miles an hour. The mountains here recede to a considerable distance from the river, and at times disappear altogether, leaving a wide valley of nicely timbered land, with here and there an occasional opening. The soil appeared to consist principally of an alluvial deposit, which had accumulated during the successive ages of time, from the debris of the mountains above. We did not go ashore to examine its character or condition particularly, and all our observations were made from the raft as we floated down the stream, but it appeared to be fertile. Here we met Mr. Andrew Holes [Hales] and four or five others of the St. Thomas party, who subsequently came down the Thompson River, returning from a prospecting tour some distance down the Fraser.[79] They washed the sand at a great many places along the shore, and examined several streams that empty into the Fraser from both sides, but they did not succeed in finding any prospects as encouraging as what we discovered upon the Athabaska.

The character of the river and of the country through which it flows continued much the same during the following two days, Wednesday and Thursday, the 3d and 4th September, interrupted only by two or three slight rapids. Our progress here was so slow that, in order to accelerate our motion, we had side oars rigged upon our raft, by means of which we doubled our speed. We also passed through, on the 4th, what the Indians had attempted to describe to us as a lake, but which was nothing more than a considerable expansion of the river. On Friday the country became more broken, and the current of the river much swifter. Hitherto our progress had been uninterrupted by any misfortune; we had been sailing steadily onward for five days, and were just beginning to entertain feelings of security, and to congratulate ourselves upon our good fortune in having escaped the dangers we dreaded. But at half-past 5 o'clock in the morning of Saturday, the 6th, we were suddenly startled by an unusual roaring noise that broke the stillness of the morning, the cause and source of which was soon explained by the lookout shouting, "Breakers ahead!"

We had reached the big rapids, and we were already so near them and were being swept toward them by the current so rapidly that we had barely time to row ashore and make fast before we were drawn into them.[80] After landing we went some distance along the shore to examine the place before we should attempt to run it. We found that the rapids consisted of three distinct stretches, with small bays or eddies of comparatively quiet water between, which had evidently been formed, at some remote period of time, by the stream breaking through as many parallel ridges. The banks on both sides are very rocky and precipitous, and the channel, which is very narrow, and obstructed in many places by pointed rocks, contained six sharp angles through which the pent-up and maddened waters rushed with violent and resistless impetuosity. It seemed like presumption to think of risking our lives through such a perilous place; but we saw no alternative, we had either to run the rapids or starve where we were. We found a passage by which we could make a portage around the first two stretches, but were unable to get over the rocky bluffs of the third.

At length Mr. Harkness decided to try it, if we would lighten the raft by a number of us making the portage, leaving only men enough aboard to man the oars. About ten men remained on the raft, and the balance of us stationed ourselves along the shore where we might possibly be able to render some assistance if it were required. Everything being ready the ropes were untied and the frail bark pushed into the current. Onward they swept like an arrow. They seemed to be rushing into the very jaws of death. Before them on the right rose a rocky reef, against which the furious flood was lashing itself into foam, threatening instant and unavoidable destruction, and on the other side a seething and eddying whirlpool was ready to engulf in its greedy vortex any mortal who might venture within its reach. With fearful velocity they were hurried along directly towards the fatal rock. Their ruin seemed inevitable. It was a moment of painful suspense. Not a word was spoken except the necessary orders of the pilot, which were distinctly heard on shore, above the din and tumult of the scene. Now was the critical moment. Every one bent manfully to his oar. The raft shot closely past the rock, tearing away the stern row-lock, and glided safely down into the eddy below. The agony was over. The gauntlet had been run, and all survived. The issue of the ordeal was announced by an involuntary cheer from the brave hearts aboard the raft, which was heartily responded to by those on shore.

The last part of the rapids was less dangerous than what we had already passed and we ran through it in safety, all hands being aboard. The scene we have described was re-enacted as each raft arrived at the canyon, and notwithstanding the imminent dangers that surrounded them, all succeeded in escaping them. Less fortunate, however, were those who attempted to run the rapids in canoes; and here the saddest part of my narrative begins.

A canoe, carrying three of the Toronto party, Messrs. Carroll, McKenzie, and Patterson, was the first to leave Tête Jaune Cache, and, as it ran considerably faster than the rafts, it arrived at the rapids two days before the first raft.[81] Those who first reached the place after them were surprised to find this party still there. Their canoe, which contained their provisions, tent, clothing, blankets, and even their coats, had foundered while they were attempting to let it down the canyon by means of a lariat, and everything belonging to them was swept away by the current. During the interval that elapsed between this occurrence and the arrival of the raft they were exposed to all the inclemency of the weather, which at the time happened to be very cold and rainy, without food, clothing, or shelter. Mr. Patterson, one of the party, had been complaining before he left the Cache, of some slight affection of the throat, which was greatly aggravated by exposure.

This canoe was followed by two others, fastened together, carrying Messrs. Robertson, Warren, and Douglas, of the Goderich party, who shared even a worse fate than those who preceded them.[82] They had only reached the first ripple when their canoes were suddenly caught by one of the whirls and capsized, throwing them and all their goods into the river. Mr. Robertson, being a good swimmer, immediately quitted the canoes and struck out for the shore, at the same time advising the others, who could not swim, to cling to them. This they found to be a very difficult matter, as the canoes were kept continually rolling over and over in the rapids. They however succeeded in maintaining their hold and as they came to the surface at each revolution of the canoes, they could see Mr. Robertson still manfully contending with the angry waves, while at each opportunity he would encourage them to hold fast, apparently more concerned for their safety than about his own welfare. At length the canoes drifted upon a shoal by which they were enabled to make a small island in the middle of the stream. After regaining their feet their first thought was to look after their companion. But he was no where to be seen. He had sunk to rise no more in this life.

He was a young man of great promise, and was universally respected throughout the company. By his general intelligence, by his kind and manly and generous deportment at all times in his daily intercourse with his fellow travelers, and by the unaffected urbanity of his manners, he won the esteem and secured the affections of every member of the company, and the tidings of his melancholy death were received by all with feelings and expressions of profound regret. And while we all deeply deplore his untimely end, we cordially sympathise with his parents and friends at home in this sad bereavement.

The remaining two threatened to be even worse, as they had no means of escaping from the island upon which they had been cast; and but for the timely arrival of the rafts of the Huntingdon party, who rescued them from their perilous situation, they must have perished also. I would fain wish that my record of fatal disasters might end here; but the chapter of accidents at this unfortunate spot is not yet concluded. Of the parties that succeeded us, two, namely: Mr. Carpenter, of Toronto, and Mr. P. Leader, of the county of Huron, Canada, were drowned by the upsetting of canoes under similar circumstances.[83]

Immediately after passing these rapids the channel again widens out and the current becomes quite sluggish. The country, too, assumes something of the same aspect as that above the canyon. So placid indeed was the stream during the whole of Saturday, and presented such a marked contrast with its turbulent character at the rapids, that we were induced to float all night. I mention this instance as an example of that condition of security, of recklessness and of blind confidence, into which men are apt to fall, who have long been accustomed to meeting dangers in various forms, and encountering difficulties of different kinds. Fancy a party of twenty-three men, who had but recently escaped so many imminent perils, and without any knowledge of the dangers that might be before them, spreading their beds on the raft and lying down to sleep, at the mercy of the current, with as much composure and as little concern for the possible consequences of such a course as though they were safely resting upon *terra firma*.

But the occurrences of the following morning awakened us to a keener sense of the risk we had been running. Daylight had scarcely dawned when we were aroused by the watch with the intelligence that the raft was running much faster than usual; and upon taking observations from objects upon the shore we discovered that we were going at a fearful velocity. We had reached a long stretch of rapids which continued for a distance of about fifteen miles; and, although there was an abundance of room while we followed the right track, and no portion of it was particularly dangerous, yet the channel was full of rocks standing here and there, which would have knocked our float into single sticks in an instant if we had chanced to run against them in the darkness of the night. Notwithstanding our caution about 8 o'clock we ran upon a sunken rock, where we stuck hard and fast until 1 o'clock. In order to extricate ourselves from this uncomfortable situation three of our party, Messrs. W.H.G. Thompson, Wood and McKenzie swam ashore, carrying with them a line which they made fast to the shore, and by means of which we drew the raft off the rock, after half cutting it in two.

After we got afloat again we proceeded without further difficulty through a tolerably open and level country, and arrived at Fort George at 8 o'clock on Monday morning, the 8th day of September. Fort George is situated on the north side of the Fraser, at the great bend, and near the mouth of Stuart's River, which flows into the Fraser from the north.[84] By the time we reached this point Mr. Patterson, who had been continually growing weaker since his severe exposure at the rapids, was found to be in a very critical condition. He was removed from the raft into the Fort where he received every attention at the hands of Dr. Stevenson and others; but the trial had been too severe, for he sank rapidly, and died at 9 o'clock in the evening of the day of our arrival. We buried him near the fort on the following day, the 9th.[85]

Slowly and sadly we laid him down.

We found a great many Indians camped near the Fort, from whom we procured some provisions, such as potatoes, turnips and berries, with bear, beaver and badger meat. We considered ourselves fortunate in meeting these natives, as our provisions were nearly out, and there was nothing for us to buy at the Fort.[86] This was the most northerly point reached during our journey. Mr. Charles, the master of Fort George, was at this time down the river for winter supplies; and, as he was hourly expected, we waited for him until Wednesday morning the 10th, being desirous of obtaining all the information we could respecting the character of the river and its mining prospects, and the distance and direction to Cariboo.[87]

As he had not arrived at this time, we started again, accompanied by an Indian whom we hired to pilot us through the rapids, which he represented as very dangerous. We reached the place at 10 o'clock, about fifteen miles below Fort George. We found the river here divided into a number of streams by huge rocks rising in the channel, against and between which the water rushed with considerable violence, but as they were far less difficult to navigate than those we had already passed, they gave us but little trouble. The channel is obstructed in this manner for a distance of half-a-mile, and the broken and rugged banks, with their overhanging cliffs, bear a striking resemblance to those of the great canyon above Fort George. The most dangerous part of it consisted of a shelving rock in the centre of the principal channel, upon which a large body of water was propelled to some distance, and, falling off at both sides, formed a double whirlpool below. All passed through them in safety. Immediately below the rapids we fell in with a company of miners, all Chinamen, who were working with rockers upon a bar on the left bank of the river.[88] These were the first mining operations we saw; but from this point all the way down the river we were continually meeting small parties working in the same manner, at intervals of every three or four miles.

We camped on Wednesday night where a party of Chinamen were working, who informed us that they were making from two to five dollars per day. On the following morning we left our moorings, and proceeded on our way in the midst of a dense fog. During the morning we passed several rapids; but as we had no previous intimation of their existence we were generally into them or through them before we had time to think whether we were going. As our course for two days had been directly southward, and as we were rapidly descending from the mountains, we observed the climate becoming perceptibly warmer.

But the happy time for which we had long been waiting at last arrived. At 2.45, P.M., on Thursday, the 11th day of September, we arrived at the Mouth of the Quesnelle, all heartily glad at having reached our destination, and delighted that so long, difficult and dangerous a journey was at length concluded.[89] But it was only after we had been allowed a little time for reflection, and had an opportunity to take a retrospective view of all the way by which we came, to consider the innumerable perils to which we had been continually exposed, through all the vicissitudes of our journey, during a period of nearly five months, and to talk of our numerous hairbreadth escapes, that we could fully realize or entirely comprehend the magnitude of the work we had accomplished.[90]

The following is a brief account of the adventures of those who came down the Thompson River, for the particulars of which we are indebted to Mr. John Fannin, of the Queenston party; Mr. R.P. Mead, of the St. Thomas party; and others. (As I have already stated, this party consisted of over twenty men, together with Mrs. Schubert and family, who came by this way for the purpose, if possible, of bringing through our horses.)

On Monday, the 1st day of September, the day upon which we left the Cache with our rafts, they crossed the river with the animals and camped on the south side of the Fraser. On the following morning, the 2d, they began their doubtful and wearisome march southward, being accompanied by a Shoushwap, who engaged to show them a trail to the head of the Thompson, and André Cardinal, our late guide, as interpreter. For the first two days after leaving the Fraser they found a tolerably good road; but after that time the Indian was unable to find a trail at all, so that they had to make one for themselves. Finding their guide of no further use to them they sent him back and trusted to the skill of André, a most faithful and intelligent guide, to pilot them safely through.[91] After toiling along for about two weeks, during which time they could only travel five or six miles a day, they reached the North Branch of the Thompson; and only those who are accustomed to making new trails through mountainous, broken and heavily timbered countries, can have any idea of the difficulties they must have encountered.

Here the mountains approach so near the river that they could proceed no further without crossing and re-crossing several times. They therefore determined to abandon all the horses except a few of the best, and to undertake to bring them down upon rafts.[92] They, accordingly, built a number of rafts and canoes, but their progress down the river was very slow as the channel was obstructed in many places by heaps of driftwood, through which they had to cut their passage. After running in this way, with variable fortune, for seven days, during which four of the party, Messrs. A. Thompson, Fannin, Hugill and W. Fortune were fast upon a snag for two days and one night without any provisions, they reached a long and impassable rapid.[93]

Here Mr. Strachan, of the London party, was drowned while attempting to swim ashore. Several others, who were also drawn into the rapids before they observed them, narrowly escaped the same fate, some by jumping ashore, and two, Messrs. Thompson and Fannin, by clinging to a rock in the middle of the stream, against which their raft was dashed

Through the Tamarac Forest

to pieces, and from which they were rescued about an hour afterward by Mr. Andrew Holes, with a canoe.[94]

Here they were obliged to make a portage of about eight miles, which was accomplished with some difficulty. Having reached the foot of the rapids they were under the necessity of constructing another set of rafts before they could proceed. While they were building these rafts a company of four miners came up the river, prospecting, from whom they received such information respecting their situation as they needed. They had only gone about forty miles with their new rafts when they came to another series of rapids, which were also impassable.[95] From this point they found a good trail to Fort Kamloops, a distance of some 120 miles, which they reached on the 11th day of October.[96] They had a very hard time of it, as their provisions were all exhausted, and but for the field of potatoes which they found by the way, some of them must have perished with hunger.

In performing this journey Mrs. Schubert has accomplished a task to which but few women are equal; and, with the additional care of three small children, one which but few *men* would have the courage to undertake. By her unceasing care for her children, by her unremitting and devoted attention to their every want, and by her never-failing solicitude about their welfare, she exemplified the nature and power of that maternal affection which prompts a mother to neglect her own comfort for the wellbeing of her child, by which she rises superior to every difficulty, and which only glows with a brighter intensity as dangers deepen around her offspring. The whole family reached Fort Kamloops in safety, and another was added to their number the day after their arrival.[97]

It now becomes my painful duty, in closing this part of my narrative, to add still another name to the long list of mortality. Mr. Frank Penwarden, of the St. Thomas party, was drowned by the upsetting of a canoe in the Thompson River, about twenty-five miles below Fort Kamloops, while his five companions were almost miraculously rescued by two Indian lads who happened to be near them.

Thus six of those who left their homes with us, whose hopes for the future were as bright, whose expectations were as boundless and whose prospects for a long life were as promising and brilliant as our own, are now numbered with the dead. The Supreme Disposer of all events, in the exercise of His inscrutable wisdom, has disappointed their earthly hopes; and I trust that those of us who were exposed to the same accidents, and who still survive the same or like dangers, will not fail to acknowledge His goodness in the preservation of our lives, and to recognise His providential care over us through all the vicissitudes of life.

The following statement will exhibit in a condensed form the total expenses of our trip, as well as the different articles of our company outfit:

Fare from Queenston to St. Paul by R.R. and Steamers,		$16.65
,, ,, St. Paul to Fort Garry by Burbank & Co.'s stages and Str. International,		$25.00
Outfit, including share of		
Tent,	$2.00	
Dishes and cooking utensils,	2.00	
Mining tools,	2.00	
Ox, cart, harness and pack-saddle,	25.00	
		$31.00
Provisions, including		
168 lbs., Flour,	$ 6.00	
50 " Pemican,	3.00	
Bacon,	1.50	
Beans, codfish and dried apples	1.50	
		$12.00
Groceries, consisting of		
Tea, Coffee, Sugar, Pepper, Salt, Mustard, Bak'g Soda, Vinegar and Matches,		
		$5.00
Incidental expenses, comprising		
payment of 4 guides,	$ 2.00	
Board at St. Paul, Georgetown and Fort Garry,	5.00	
Charges for use of H.B. Boats, &c.,	1.00	
		$ 8.00
Total expenses,		$97.65

Our mining tools were the only articles in the above list that we found to be unnecessary. They were also very troublesome to carry, particularly after we began packing, and the price of them would have been much more judiciously expended in an additional supply of groceries.

The following table of distances has been calculated from a system of dead-reckoning which we adopted, and does not pretend to be absolutely correct, and should therefore be accepted with some allowances; but from the scrupulous care with which a record of our daily progress was

kept, it is believed that this computation will be found to be a very close
approximation to the actual distances.[98] That portion of it between Fort
Garry and Tête Jaune Cache cannot vary more than a few miles at most,
but the data from which we estimated the distances down the Fraser are
more liable to error, since the current flows much faster in some places
than in others and it is very difficult to arrive at an average rate upon
which to base a calculation.

		Whole No. of days on the road.	No. days of actual travel.	Distances
From	Queenston to St. Paul,	5 days	4 days	900 miles
''	St. Paul to Georgetown,	11	5	320
''	Georgetown to Fort Garry,	18	6	430
	Totals by public conveyance	34	15	1650
''	Fort Garry to Fort Ellice,	19	12	250
''	Ft. Ellice to Touchwood Hills,	9	7	172
''	Touchwood Hills to South Saskatchewan,	7	6	125
''	South Saskatchewan to Carlton House,	1	1	18
''	Carlton House to Ft. Pitt,	8	7	153
''	Ft. Pitt to Edmonton House,	12	9	200
	Total distance with carts,	56	42	918
''	Edmonton House to Pembina River,	14	6	95
''	Pembina to McLeod's River,	5	5	86
''	McLeod's R. to foot of Mts.,	9	7	135
''	Foot of Mountains to Tête Jaune Cache	9	9	143
	Total dist. with pack horses	37	27	459
''	Tête Jaune Cache to the Big Rapids,	9	5	280

"	Big Rapids to Fort George,	3	3	155
"	Fort George to Mouth of Quesnelle	3	2	85
	Total distance with rafts,	15	10	520
	Grand totals, Queenston to Quesnelle	142	94	3547

It is rather unfortunate for our present purpose that we were not provided with some philosophical instruments with which we might have taken more extensive and accurate observations of the climate, its temperature, humidity, &c., of the altitude of the mountains and the elevation at different points of the road by which we came over them, with the grades in ascending and descending the various slopes; of the currents of the different streams, and other matters respecting this Territory that are likely soon to become of paramount importance. The facts that have been given in the foregoing account were gathered merely from personal observation, and are consequently liable to inaccuracies.

Although the journey was performed at considerable sacrifice of time, and unfortunately with loss of life also, and is not likely to be attended with any direct personal advantage to those who survived it; yet, in a public and national sense, I think we may reasonably entertain a hope that it will not be without a practical and beneficial effect. It has at all events demonstrated the practicability of the route, not only for men but for horses and oxen also, some of which were brought through by both Fraser River and Thompson River routes. It will also serve to awaken public attention in Canada, the country that would be most directly benefited by the opening up and colonization of this territory, since every corner of Canada was represented in our company, numbers of which will convey to every neighborhood some goodly report of the land.

The mineral resources of this region, which have been merely hinted at in the preceding pages, in connection with the rich deposits that are known to exist upon the western side of the mountains, may yet place this territory in the vanguard of the nations, when once they are fully developed. But it is to its agricultural capacity that I wish at this time to invite special attention. During our journey across this territory we followed, as nearly as we could judge, making due allowance for the advance of the season, an isothermal line of the northern counties of Western Canada. On both sides of our trail, but particularly on the south side, between our path and the 49th parallel, are tens of thousands of acres of the most fertile land which, in the exuberance of its productions, even in a state of nature, almost rivals tropical vegetation. In a sanitary point of view I think it will not suffer from a comparison with the most favored sections of the world. That so large a company, selected at random and without any special reference to soundness of constitution, some of whom, indeed, were suffering from chronic diseases, which were greatly alleviated or entirely removed, should be exposed to all the hardships necessarily encountered upon such a trip, for so long a period of time, without a single man, even for a day, upon the sick list, is certainly very remarkable, and is a standing proof of the healthfulness and salubrity of the climate.[99]

Why, then, should the crowded cities of Europe still continue to be overburdened with a redundant population, while upwards of *two hundred thousand square miles* of such land, with such a desirable climate, are lying waste and uncultivated and inviting occupation? Besides, but few of the hardships incident to the early settlement of heavily timbered countries would here be encountered. Here a home is already prepared for the pioneers of the country. The fields are ready for putting in the plough, while the immense herds of buffaloes that feed upon the plains would furnish a certain and abundant supply of food until a crop could be gathered from the soil. The scarcity of timber for building purposes in many localities would no doubt be an impediment to the settlement of the country; but the great rivers already described— the great arteries which contain the very life-blood of the territory—rise in regions densely covered with magnificent timber, whence it could easily be floated to nearly every corner of the land. The hostility of the various Indian tribes, upon whose hunting grounds settlements would necessarily encroach, may be urged as another difficulty. We did entertain grave apprehensions upon this point before we set out upon our journey, and armed ourselves accordingly; but we found the red men of the prairies to be our best friends, and before we reached the end of our trip we were only too glad to meet them.

But if the country we have attempted to describe is really so desirable, the question would immediately arise, what facilities for transportation would an immigrant here be likely to meet with? I answer that, when once in the country, natural facilities sufficient for the want of a young colony already exist. In the first place the level and unbroken nature of the country presents but very few obstructions to the progress of wheeled carriages in any direction, and almost to any distance that may be desired. Then, Lake Winnipeg and the Great Saskatchewan Rivers offer an almost unbroken line of communication from the Selkirk Settlement to the foot of the Rocky Mountains. Again, the Assiniboine and Qu'Appelle Rivers on the south of this line, and the Pembina, McLeod's and Athabaska on the north, with numerous subsidiary streams, divide the whole North-West Territory into convenient sections. A line of communication following Lake Winnipeg and the North Branch of the Saskatchewan to the Acton House and thence across the mountains, by the Vermillion Pass, has already been described in one of the maps accompanying the report of the exploring expedition sent out by the Canadian Government, in 1858. After passing over the ground I can see no insuperable obstacle to the carrying out of the designs therein contemplated. But another route, involving still less land travel, might be obtained by pursuing the lines indicated on the map as far as the Edmonton House; thence by land to the Pembina, a distance, according to our estimates, of 95 miles; thence by the Pembina and Athabaska Rivers to the upper crossing of the Athabaska, from which point a wagon road could easily be built to Tête Jaune Cache, a distance, by the trail, of a little over 100 miles, making 200 miles in all. From the Cache the Fraser is navigable the whole way into Cariboo, with the exception of the rapids we have previously described, around which short portage roads might be constructed with but little difficulty.

In thus pointing out these different roads across the continent, I do not wish to be understood as recommending, or in the least degree encouraging, the "Overland Route" as a means merely of reaching the gold fields of British Columbia, in the present condition of the country. It is certainly cheap, healthy and practicable; but these advantages are more than counterbalanced by the difference of time between this and the ocean route. The only obstacle, then, that prevents the immediate occupation and settlement of this magnificent tract of country, is the want of proper communication between the Red River Colony and Canada, and a sufficient outlet for its bountiful and munificent productions. But let sufficient transit facilities be established between Fort Garry and Fort William; let the flood gates once be lifted between Lake Superior and Lake Winnipeg, and a living stream would immediately pour in which would soon overflow the whole land. The wonder is that the tide of immigration has been so long restrained. Then, this preliminary step having been taken in the right direction, the great, crowning work, towards the achievement of which the attention of thousands is at the present time eagerly directed—the construction of a great inter-oceanic railway that will connect the Atlantic with the Pacific—will follow as a national necessity.

Many of the apparent difficulties that at present surround the accomplishment of this gigantic enterprise are owing to the distance of the standpoint from which all our observations are taken. But let the light of science and civilization shine in upon the proposed track and these obstacles will speedily disappear. If, then, as present appearances indicate, this vast interjacent territory be destined to become the very heart and centre of the great British American Empire, that will unite in one grand confederation the present widely separated provinces, it is alike the duty and interest of all parties concerned to pursue towards it such a line of policy as will most surely and effectually hasten the accomplishment of so desirable an end. Then our highly favored country will take its place among the nations, and become one of the great highways for the commerce of the world. Then Canada, our home, with her golden fields, and Columbia, the land of our adoption, with her fields of gold, shall become one and the same country, indissolubly united by a common nationality, and cemented by a community of commercial interests—one of the strongest links in that chain which binds together the great brotherhood of nations.

That this may be the proud destiny of our common country, and that we may be privileged in our own day to witness its glorious consummation, is the earnest wish of

Your obedient servant,

THOS. MCMICKING.

Plate 7. Thomas McMicking (1829-66), the leader of the largest single group of people to travel across the Canadian prairies to British Columbia before the building of the railway. **PABC**

Plate 8. A self-portrait by the artist William G.R. Hind (1833-89) painted about 1865. Hind was a member of the Redgrave party which followed a few weeks behind the major group of Overlanders. **PABC**

Plate 9. Queenston, Canada West, where McMicking organized his original company of twenty-four men from the Niagara and St. Catherines area.   Ontario Archives

Plate 10. The steamer *Frank Steele* (centre) on which the Overlanders travelled from La Crosse to St. Paul. In his account, McMicking bitterly protested the treatment his party received at the hands of the ship's officers.   Minnesota Historical Society

Plate 11. Upper Fort Garry, where the Overlanders purchased their horses, oxen, carts and supplies. They also consulted with officials and others about the route they should follow and engaged a guide.   Hudson's Bay Company

Plate 12. The *International*, the second steamboat on the Red River, tied up in the Assiniboine at the Fort Garry Warehouse. The Overlanders were passengers on her maiden voyage from Georgetown to the Fort, which began ten days late and took six days instead of the two they expected.   Hudson's Bay Company

Plate 13. Watercolour by W.G.R. Hind showing the miners leaving Fort Garry. The large wheels of the Red River carts gave them good clearance over rough terrain.   PAC

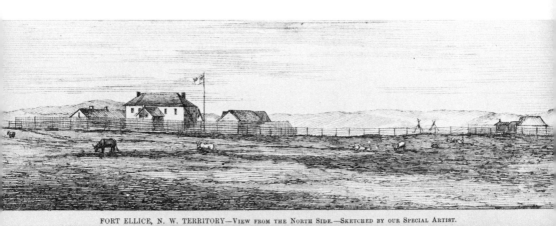

FORT ELLICE, N. W. TERRITORY—VIEW FROM THE NORTH SIDE.—SKETCHED BY OUR SPECIAL ARTIST.

Plate 14. Fort Ellice on the Assiniboine from an engraving in the *Canadian Illustrated News.* The timbers for the erection of these buildings were being prepared when the parties camped here on 14 and 15 June 1862.   Hudson's Bay Company

ate 15. At Fort Pitt, having been deserted by their first guide, the Overlanders hired an Iroquois named Michel to lead them on the
il to Edmonton.   Hudson's Bay Company

ate 16. Untitled picture of Plains Indians by W.G.R. Hind. When they began their trip, the travellers were apprehensive about
ssible raids on their animals. However, by the end, McMicking declared they had found them ''to be our best friends…we were
ly too glad to meet with them.''   PABC

Plate 17. At Fort Edmonton, the miners had to decide on their route over the mountains. After much discussion, they finally decided on the Leather (Yellowhead) pass and hired André Cardinal as their guide.   Provincial Archives of Alberta

Plate 18. Painting of the Leather Pass by W.G.R. Hind. Though the miners left many of their oxen at Edmonton, some were brought through the mountains.   McCord Museum, McGill University, Montreal

Plate 19. Stephen Redgrave (1831-1903), the leader of the Toronto party with which the artist Hind travelled. Born and educated in England, Redgrave was a police sergeant in Toronto before the expedition. In British Columbia he held a number of government positions.   PABC

Plate 20. Catherine Schubert (1835-1918), the only woman in the group. She gave birth to her second daughter, Rose, the day after the Thompson River party reached Kamloops.   PABC

Plate 21. Robert Burns McMicking (1843-1915), Thomas's younger brother, one of the many Overlanders who remained in British Columbia and became prominent in the early business community. PABC

Plate 22. A.L. Fortune from Huntingdon, Lower Canada, was a member of McMicking's governing committee on the trip. Since he had studied for the ministry, he conducted many of the Sunday services. In later years, he did missionary work among the Indians of the North Okanagan.   PABC

Plate 23. R.H. Alexander (1844-1915) joined Redgrave's group, and his published *Diary and Narrative* of the journey records hardships all the parties shared. He became one of the founders of the city of Vancouver.   PABC

CHEAP
Board and Lodgings
AT
$8.00 .... per week.
1.00 .... per day.
DINNER .... 5 bits.
SUPPER OR BREAKFAST .... 2 bits.

AT THE
Overland Restaurant,
Broad street, near Fort street.

mh2 1m°   FORTUNE & MORROW

Plate 24. The advertisement for the Overland Restaurant opened by A.L. Fortune and William Morrow on Broad Street in Victoria in March, 1863. In 1864, they returned to the Cariboo. Victoria *Colonist*

Plate 25. Most of the Overlanders did not remain in the Cariboo for any length of time. They either returned home or settled in other parts of British Columbia. Those who, like McMicking, moved to New Westminster would have had many occasions to visit this building, which served as Land Registry, Post Office, and Assay Office for many years. Special Collections, UBC Library

Appendix 1

A Note on the McMicking Family

Information about TM's ancestors and some of his descendants has been derived mainly from family papers in the possession of Robert Burns McMicking's great-grandson, Ronald Bruce McMicking of Victoria. Ronald and his wife Linda Graves McMicking opened their home and spent several hours in conversation with me and more hours at work clarifying and checking details contained in the documents. A sketch of the family crest found among the papers displays two fitting mottoes for this and other generations of the family: "Res non Verba" and "We Hae Dune."

The following untitled note, dated 15 February 1925, was written by TM's sister, Emma Louise McMicking Dennis, youngest child of William and Mary McMicking. It contains the essence of family tradition regarding the history of the McMickings before the time of Thomas McMicking "the Third," TM's great-grandfather.

The McMicking family represents the old Ayrshire and Wigtonshire McMickings. The McMickings of Killantringan [held] one of the most ancient baronies of Ayrshire and at various epochs of Scottish history were not undistinguished. One of their members, in 1427, lost his life through his adherence to the Lord of the Isles in a rebellion against King James of Scotland. At the Reformation the family took a prominent part in Ayrshire and during the reign of Charles II many of them suffered imprisonment and fines in the cause of civil and religious liberty. Sir Gilbert McMicking married Agnes MacDonald, daughter of John, Son of Angus, Lord of the Isles. Major Gilbert McMicking, C.M.G., of Miltonise, Wigtonshire, Scotland, who sat in the Imperial House for a number of years

and who commanded the Royal Scots during the Great War, and
Admiral Sir James Startin, are all members of this family.

"A Sketch of the Life of Thomas McMicking (the Fourth)," written
by James McMicking (1811-91), "his youngest son," is undated. James
McMicking was TM's uncle. Much of the information his sketch
provides is corroborated by various census and municipal records from
the Stamford area, as well as by newspaper articles and records of the
Ontario Historical Society which mention the family.

According to James McMicking, little was known about TM's great-
grandfather, Thomas III (d. 1756), except that he was "a religious man"
and a blacksmith, who lived in the parish of Stranraer, Galloway (now
Wigtown), Scotland, and was married twice. His second wife was Janet
Mulwain, with whom he had four children, including Thomas IV
(1750-1830), TM's grandfather. Thomas IV became a stonemason in
Scotland but gave up his trade when he emigrated to New York. He took
up land near the Catskill Mountains on the Delaware River with his
brother John, and there made a home for his mother and one widowed
sister, Janet Cooper, and her two sons. In 1776 during the Revolutionary
War, the family, except for Janet Mulwain McMicking, was taken
prisoner by the Seneca Indians. Thomas IV is said to have remained in
captivity for four years, but eventually he escaped and made his way to
Fort Niagara, where he served with a British fatigue regiment for about a
year. About 1783, after discharge, he was given a grant of two hundred
acres of land, Lots 1 and 2 in the township of Stamford, as a reward for
his Loyalist activities.

The *Papers and Records* of the Ontario Historical Society (vol. 25
[1929]: 308-12) indicate a slightly different version of the facts of Thomas
IV's life between 1771 and 1783. As "T. McMeeking" he filed a claim at
Niagara in 1788 for property losses in the Revolution, and he stated that
he came to America in 1774 and took up land at the "W. Branch,
Delaware River, Tryon Co., N. York." He testified, and his evidence was
supported by military witnesses, that he "frequently furnished [Brant
and other British commanders and their parties] with provisions and
intelligence," for which he was imprisoned by the rebels. In 1780 he was
taken prisoner by the Senecas and brought to Canada, and starting in
1781 he served at Niagara with Colonel Guy Johnson's Foresters for one
year.

All records agree that after 1783, at Niagara, Thomas IV again made a
home for his mother, sister, and nephews. In 1787 he made a journey
back to Scotland where he married Isabella Gass (1767-1830), daughter
of William Gass, a grain merchant of Annandale, Dumfries. Thomas IV
and Isabella had ten children. During the war of 1812, the family farm

lay between several battlefields. Thomas IV was sixty-two years old but still hale enough to fight in the battle of Queenston Heights.

William (1805-57), TM's father, was the eighth child and second son of Thomas IV and Isabella Gass. When William McMicking became old enough, he took over the family farm, and in 1827 he married Mary McClellan (1808-73) who was one of the thirteen children of John McClellan and his wife Jane Thompson.

TM's maternal grandfather John McClellan, a member of a family reputed to be related to U.S. generals George B. McClellan and Ulysses Grant, was also a Loyalist and had received a grant of land situated about seven miles from the McMicking home. Emma Dennis reported that about 1835 John McClellan "sold his farm and went a hundred miles farther back, to a place called Caledon," where he later died at the age of 96.

TM's father, William McMicking, was, according to his daughter Emma, "a most successful farmer, and a thorough Christian, Elder in the Presbyterian Church at Stamford that his father helped to organize." He was a justice of the peace and a captain in the Loyalist Militia, serving during the rebellion of 1837.

An extract from "an old Family Bible dated at Stamford, Dec. 31, 1842," in the "possession of John McMicking, R.R. 2, Hamilton, Ont.," contains the following information about TM and his brothers and sisters, the twelve children of William and Mary McMicking:

Jane (29 February 1828—5 December 1881), m. William Parker.
Thomas (16 April 1829—25 August 1866), m. Laura Chubbuck.
Isabella (4 January 1831—6 June 1911), m. John Parker.
John (10 October 1832—21 December 1896), m. Emily Gilchrist.
William (25 August 1834—20 December 1912), m. Mary McDermit.
James R. (1 April 1836—14 September 1917), m. Martha McBerlie.
Eleanor (26 March 1838—7 May 1886), m. James Haggert.
Mary E. (30 July 1840—18 February 1909), m. James Parker.
Robert Burns (7 July 1843—27 November 1915), m. Margaret
    Leighton.
Sarah (21 November 1846—19 November 1926), m. Hugh Mitchele.
George A. (25 May 1849—15 September 1921), m. Mary Bowen.
Emma Louise (25 November 1851—3 January 1934), m. Mr. Dennis.

TM married Laura Chubbuck on 7 July 1854 according to the *Niagara Chronicle.* Emma Dennis gave the date as 12 July 1853, but her memory has apparently failed her on this point. Laura, born in 1835, was the daughter of Job Chubbuck, "a well-to-do merchant" who about 1840 built a well-known Queenston landmark once known as the Chubbuck block. Here TM had his general dealership in partnership with one of his wife's relatives, probably his father-in-law Job "Chubbick," who is listed as a "general merchant" in the 1865 Lincoln County Directory. The Chubbuck block was probably the same building later known as the "Fisher block" because it came to be owned by Carl Fisher, who married TM's daughter Laura Augusta. The building was not demolished until 1968. Further details of its history can be found in an article entitled "Queenston Landmark Is Disappearing," by Francis Petrie (*Niagara Falls Evening Review*, 28 July 1968).

TM and Laura McMicking had five children:

Thomas A., b. 1856, d. 2 August 1879, at Victoria, B.C. Thomas was apparently visiting his uncle Robert's family when he died of Bright's disease. Emma Dennis stated that he was in Victoria at the invitation of his mother's brother, Samuel Chubbuck, but this appears unlikely. M.S. Wade claims that Samuel Chubbuck had left British Columbia in 1863 and settled shortly thereafter in the United States.

Laura Augusta, b. 1857, m. (i) Arthur Henry; one son, Lee; (ii) 1916, Carl Fisher. In 1923 Laura, known as "Guss," was living in St. Catharines with her second husband.

William Francis, or Frank, b. 1860, d. 25 August 1866. He was drowned together with his father TM.

Robert Lincoln, b. 1862. In 1925 Robert was living in Detroit.

Samuel Chubbard, or Chubbuck, b. 1865, d. 1875. His aunt Emma Dennis stated that he died at Queenston of "an abscess on the side of his neck" and was buried in the cemetery at Stamford.

After the death of TM and Frank at New Westminster, Laura McMicking returned with her remaining children to Queenston and took rooms in the Chubbuck block. She lived there until her children were grown, and she died in March 1923 at the home of her daughter Laura in St. Catharines.

Some additional information on the career of Robert Burns McMicking may be of interest to British Columbians. Robert was educated at Stamford, as was his older brother, TM, but Robert was forced to leave school early because of the death of his father. According to one account, he went to work at the age of thirteen for the Montreal Telegraph Company at Queenston. The 1861 Stamford Township census indicates that at this time Robert was living at home with his widowed mother, Mary, and four older and three younger siblings. He continued to work for the Telegraph Company until his departure for British Columbia in 1862.

After their quick journey from the mouth of the Quesnel River to Lightning Creek in the Cariboo district in the fall of 1862, immediately after their arrival in the colony, Robert and TM returned to Quesnel and then made their way to New Westminster. TM apparently went down directly, but Robert lingered, working as a cook and then as a labourer on a roadbuilding gang operating near Bridge Creek and Lac la Hache. He then followed his brother, travelling by the Lillooet-Harrison Lake route, and arrived in New Westminster on 16 November 1862.

After spending the winter doing odd jobs, Robert was hired by W.J. Armstrong to work in his grocery store and remained there from 1863 to 1865. He then took a job with the Collins Overland Telegraph Company, which was building a line through northern British Columbia. The company intended to continue the line across Alaska, the Bering Strait, Siberia, and Russia to Europe. Robert McMicking was in charge of the Quesnel office when the order came to abandon the work beyond that point at the news of the successful completion of the second Atlantic cable in 1866. When Thomas McMicking was drowned at New Westminster, Robert returned to that city, and then took up a position as manager of the Yale telegraph office. In 1869 he married Margaret Leighton, niece of Thomas Buie, J.P. at Lytton. In 1870 Robert was transferred to Victoria where he took charge of the Western Union office. The following year he became superintendent of the B.C. Government Telegraph Services, with headquarters at Yale, where he also served as police magistrate, J.P., and coroner. After transfer back to Victoria, he left the telegraph service in 1880 to help found and manage the Victoria and Esquimalt Telephone Company. One of the first two telephones in British Columbia was installed in his home. The telephone company prospered, and Robert McMicking went on to help found companies which introduced electric light to city streets (1883) and to homes and businesses (1887) and brought fire alarm systems to Victoria and later to the whole province. He was known for his engineering and mechanical ability and once invented a lightweight telegraph line insulator.

Robert McMicking and his wife had seven children who survived infancy, and many of their descendants still live in Victoria and other parts of British Columbia. Robert McMicking died 27 November 1915. J.A. Mara, another Overlander and well-known British Columbian, was one of the honorary pallbearers. For more information on Robert McMicking, see his "Journal"; Kerr, *Biographical Dictionary*, pp. 253-61; Wade, *Overlanders*, pp. 159-60; Robert McMicking's obituary, *Colonist*, 28 November 1915; "Pioneer of Victoria Helped to Pave the Course of Progress," *Colonist*, 3 December 1922.

Appendix 2

A Note on the Trail

Most of the Overlanders used Red River carts to carry their goods and possessions between Fort Garry and Fort Edmonton. The Red River cart was built for the prairie and the prairie trails were developed, to an extent, to suit the cart. Readers may therefore be interested in the following information, which will serve to supplement TM's description of the vehicle. The details are taken from various sources, including Hargrave's *Red River*, Russell's *Carlton Trail*, Hind's *Sketch of an Overland Route to British Columbia*, Howard's *Strange Empire*, as well as the other Overlander "journals."

Hargrave accurately describes how the carts were made by the Métis, who used them so much that they were known to the prairie Indians by a sign which meant "half wagon, half man."

> [The carts] are constructed entirely of wood, without any iron whatever, the axles and rims of the wheels forming no exception to the rule. Although this might at first sight appear a disadvantage, as denoting a want of strength, it is really the reverse, because, in the country traversed by these vehicles, wood is abundant, and always to be obtained in quantities sufficient to mend any breakages which might take place. The only tools necessary, not only to mend but to construct a cart, are an axe, a saw, a screw-auger and a draw-knife; with these the traveller is independent, so far as regards the integrity of his conveyance. Indeed, the cart may be described as a light box frame poised upon an axle connecting two strong wooden wheels. . . . The harness is very rude, and is made of dressed ox-hide.

Each cart is drawn by an ox, and in cases where speed is an object a horse is substituted (*Red River*, pp. 58-59).

The felloes of the wheels were wrapped with rawhide which bound the rims tightly together as it dried, and the wheels could be removed and loaded in the box or attached at the sides or underneath, so that the cart could be floated across rivers. Although the carts were relatively small and light, allowing them to be easily manoeuvred and extricated from mud and deep sand, the wheels themselves were large, giving clearance over rough terrain: "5 feet 3 inches high made every way the same as the Wheels are in Canada, only about one third heavier, the fellows are 3½ inches deep & 3 inches wide so as not to cut into the sod the rest of the wheel is made in proportion, while the boddy is made precisely the same as the French Canadian cart" (Sellar, "Journal," p. 21). The height of the wheels also allowed the owner to sleep sheltered beneath the box at night.

Many old illustrations and present-day replicas show the Red River cart uncovered, but it could be and often was covered with canvas stretched upon a frame arching above the box. Dobson Prest, another member of TM's company, noted in a letter written to his mother from Edmonton (22 July 1862) that "our train is a mile long, and two thirds of our carts being covered, make us look like an awful army." According to John Hunniford, while at Fort Garry the Overlanders themselves covered the carts they had bought there ("Journal," p. 4). From a distance, as can be seen in some of W.G.R. Hind's illustrations, the carts resembled the American covered wagons used on the Oregon Trail, but at closer range their smaller size and two rather than four wheels distinguished them.

Indian ponies could cover 80 to 100 kilometres a day while pulling "light" loads of 180 to 270 kilograms, and oxen pulling heavier carts— 360 to 400 kilograms—were expected to average 32 kilometres daily if given a rest during the noon heat. As TM notes, the Overlanders soon found that the longer the noontime rest, the more their animals could eat and the better they fared. The men concluded also that they might have packed lighter loads on the carts in order to gain extra speed. On good terrain, however, such as that between Fort Ellice and the Touchwood Hills, the Overlanders actually made close to 40 kilometres per day, and over the whole distance with carts they averaged 35 kilometres for every ten hours' travel. This pace was easily sustained by man as well as beast, and although the carts could be driven while the owners sat or stood in them, most operators, including the Overlanders, walked beside their "outfits."

Hargrave's comment about wood for repair of the carts being

plentiful everywhere did not apply to portions of the Overlanders' trail. Sellar observed that Portage la Prairie marked the "end of Oak timbered land so we lay over for a few hours for the purpose of laying in a stock of wheel fellows & spoaks, & Exaltrees, to do us till we would arrive at Fort Edmonton on the Saskatchewan" ("Journal," p. 34). In an emergency, other wood besides oak could be used for repairs, but there were places where no trees of any kind grew, such as the region just west of the Touchwood Hills. There the trekkers had to carry wood even for their cooking fires.

In large cart trains, as R.C. Russell observes, the wagons did not follow each other single file unless compelled by the nature of the terrain, or unless the trail was unusually hard and dry.

> When freighters were traveling along the trail with long strings of heavily loaded carts, each man looked after several units, a unit consisting of one pony or ox and one cart. Each freighter drove the animal hitched to his leading cart and tied the next succeeding animal to a rear corner of this cart, so that the animal walked in the rut of the wheel in front of it. Each succeeding animal under the driver's care followed in the wheel track of the cart immediately ahead. As a result of this arrangement, the carts did not travel in a single line but were spread out so that the trail consisted of as many as sixteen ruts all worn to about the same depth. This method reduced the danger of the ruts becoming too deep for convenient use and lessened the chances of getting stuck in wet spots on the prairie. The old cart trails differed in appearance from the trails made at a later date by wagons, buckboards and buggies. The latter trails consisted of two wheel marks and a path for single horses between them (*Carlton Trail*, pp. 1-2).

Since each Overlander cart had at least one operator, and in most cases two, there would have been no need to tie wagons together, but it is probable that for the reasons outlined by Russell, TM's company drove several units abreast of each other wherever possible.

The Overlanders' path between Fort Garry and Carlton House and beyond, by extension, to Edmonton, was known as the Carlton Trail. Before discussing the general nature of that trail, and, later, the specific route taken by TM's party through what is now Saskatchewan, I must acknowledge with gratitude my debt to Warren Clubb of the Saskatchewan Archives Board at Saskatoon. Mr. Clubb shared with great generosity and enthusiasm his expert knowledge of the prairie trail network in the nineteenth century.

Changing conditions on the prairie caused the position of the trails to shift from year to year and even within the same year. Mr. Clubb has pointed out that the cart route generally kept to high rather than low ground, especially in wet seasons. In unusually dry times, however, travellers tended to skirt more closely the margins of those temporarily shrunken lakes and sloughs in the direct line of march. Again, the fording places at large streams sometimes shifted by hundreds of metres or even several kilometres from one season to another, as sandbars appeared and disappeared, old channels were filled up, or parts of the river shore washed away leaving only steep overhanging banks offering no convenient access to the water. The changing circumstances of human history also altered the trails, for example, when trading posts were built, re-built, abandoned, or moved.

Our knowledge of the exact location of the old routes is not complete. Maps used in 1862, such as those published with the reports of the Palliser and H.Y. Hind exploring expeditions, show the major river crossings and HBC posts, but between these points, they give only a general idea of the major trails. Written descriptions in these reports and in the Overlander documents themselves are helpful but often sketchy. Some of the place names mentioned by TM and his companions in their accounts are no longer known and cannot be found in old gazetteers. In many cases it has been possible to identify these positively by a process of deduction and elimination; other times the modern designations given here are educated guesses. It is true that after 1862 the early surveyors marked the cart trails where they saw them, and their maps are invaluable to the modern researcher, but they cannot be relied on. Sometimes wheel ruts had disappeared where parts of the trail had fallen into disuse, or new branches leading to pioneer settlements were shown as part of the old network when in fact they had not existed in fur trade days. There are spots, such as at Fort Carlton on the hill above the reconstructed post, where traces of the old ruts can still be seen, but elsewhere one can rarely be certain that one is standing where the Overlanders passed.

The following remarks therefore represent a tentative description of their probable route with reference to modern towns, highways, and railways and have been arrived at by a species of detective work which involved consulting the old maps and documents mentioned here and large-scale modern maps, and books which mention the old trails, such as those by Irene Spry, J.G. MacGregor, and R.C. Russell; and by discussion with a number of interested historians and archivists from Manitoba to British Columbia.

Upon leaving Fort Garry, the Overlanders proceeded by the cart trail up the northwest side of the Assiniboine River to Sturgeon Creek and continued the next day to White Horse Plain and Lane's Post, an HBC store at Pigeon Lake, about forty kilometres from the fort. The next drive brought them to Long Lake, which lies about five kilometres south of modern High Bluff near the northernmost bend of the Assiniboine. Here they stopped to organize themselves and elected TM leader of the expedition. They then moved on to Portage la Prairie, where the Carlton Trail divided. The northern branch veered northwestward to pass near present Westbourne, Woodside, Gladstone, Neepawa, and Minnedosa. The Overlanders appear to have taken the southern branch, or the "middle cart trail" as it was termed by Richard Alexander, a member of Redgrave's company of Overlanders, presumably to distinguish it from yet more southerly trails which led not to Carlton House but to the Souris River region and U.S. territory.

This "middle" trail is shown on a number of early maps of Manitoba, including Edouard Deville's Map of Part of Western Canada, 1883; Robert Richardson's Map of the Province of Manitoba, 1882; and a number of government maps of the province up to at least 1912. On Deville's map it is labelled "Saskatchewan Road." It led west from Portage la Prairie just north of the present Trans-Canada Highway. In the vicinity of Bagot the trail dipped slightly southwest, crossed to the south side of Highway 1, passed south of MacGregor, ran west to Austin where it crossed Squirrel Creek, then southwest to Sidney, west along the modern highway to Pine Creek north of Melbourne, and here veered northwest to pass between Harte and Gregg. It crossed the Whitemud River south of Oberon, passed five to seven kilometres west of Cordova, and crossed the Minnedosa River, or Little Saskatchewan as TM called it, a few kilometres west of the modern town of Minnedosa.

According to R.C. Russell, the trail rejoined its northern spur thirty-two kilometres west and eight kilometres north of Minnedosa, which would put the junction slightly southwest of Newdale, or about half-way between present-day Basswood and Salt Lake. The trail continued on to the southern end of Salt Lake, west again to the southern end of Shoal Lake and beyond to crossings on the Arrow River, Minnewasta Creek and Birdtail Creek near modern Birtle. From here a short westerly drive brought the caravan to Fort Ellice on Beaver Creek near its junction with the Assiniboine, where there is now an historic site close to the Manitoba-Saskatchewan border.

From this point the trail turned northwest to cross the Qu'Appelle River, then ran up along the Qu'Appelle to the vicinity of Welby (somewhere northwest of which the company's first guide, Charles Rochette, deserted them), thence northwest along Cutarm Creek to a point about eighteen kilometres north and three east of Esterhazy. Turning west it passed along Kaposvar Creek to a point about twenty-nine kilometres south of Melville, thence to points just south of Fenwood and Goodeve. Northwest of Melville the trail passed through or very close to the sites of Hubbard, Ituna, and Jasmin, slightly north of Kelliher, Leross, Lestock, Touchwood, and Punnichy, through the Poor

Man Indian Reserve in the Touchwood Uplands, on to Lanigan, south of Humboldt Lake, past Carmel, Marie Lake, and a point about one and a half kilometres south of Wakaw. Continuing on south of St. Julien and through the southwest corner of the Arrow Indian Reserve, the Overlanders were led to a major crossing place on the South Saskatchewan River near Batoche.

From here the trail ran along the north side of Duck Lake to the crossing place of the North Saskatchewan River at Carlton House, a short day's drive of twenty-nine kilometres. (It was between the crossing places of the south and north branches that the Redgrave company of Overlanders, following about twelve days behind TM's party at this point, left the trail followed by the earlier group to take a path which led south of the Elbow of the North river and through the Eagle Hills to the vicinity of present North Battleford, striking the "regular" trail to Edmonton two weeks later where it crossed the Vermilion River.) After crossing to the north side of the North Saskatchewan, TM's company continued to a point just north of Blaine Lake, west from there to the vicinity of Gordon Lake, Redfield, and Hatherleigh, south of Jackfish Lake (or Pike Lake as Robert McMicking calls it; he also mentions that the company lost their way the day before reaching this large lake, so the trail cannot have been well-marked in this region). From here the cart train travelled up the Turtlelake River to the vicinity of Dulwich, turned west to pass the North Saskatchewan again near Butte-St-Pierre, and crossed near Paradise Hill and Frenchman Butte to Fort Pitt.

At Fort Pitt a new guide, "Michel," was hired; he led the party back to the south side of the river and, according to TM, along the valley of the North Saskatchewan all the way to Edmonton. The river was not always in sight, however, and even the experienced Michel lost his way at one point, the trail being very indistinct in places. No special landmarks are mentioned by any of TM's party (except the crossing place of Vermilion River), so little else can be said to help the reader locate the trail in this area today.

Most of the ox-carts and oxen were exchanged at Fort Edmonton for pack-horses, but some Overlanders were unwilling or unable to get horses and retained their oxen as pack-animals. A few purchased mules. As TM notes, the animals were able to carry between sixty-seven and 112 kilograms each, and some of the travellers used more than one animal. Over the total distance with pack-horses to Tête Jaune Cache, the party made an average of twenty-seven kilometres a day.

West of Edmonton, the trail was again very faint and often disappeared in muskeg, where the animals got mired, or in heavy bush through which the men had to hack a path. Early twentieth-century maps of Alberta do show some trails in the general area through which the Overlanders passed, but there is no certainty that these were in use in

1862. Fortunately, TM gives many details of landmarks and placenames here. When the later maps seem to indicate a different route from that suggested by TM or by the author of *Overland by the Yellowhead*, J.G. MacGregor (who mentions the McMicking party's guide from Edmonton, Andre Cardinal, as a pioneer of the 1862 trail between that fort and Jasper), the written evidence has been preferred.

The first day's journey brought the Overlanders to St. Albert at Big Lake, and the third day to the Catholic mission at Lac Ste Anne. After leaving Lac Ste Anne, they crossed the Sturgeon River and passed Isle Lake (TM's "Lake of Many Hills") on the north side, then they crossed the Pembina River and continued west along the Lobstick River (TM's "Buffalo-dung River") to a ford east of Chip Lake at about the point where the Lobstick turns north. After passing Chip Lake on the south side, they turned slightly northwest along the Lobstick to another crossing place, possibly north of Niton, and travelled west of here to cross Carrot River (TM's "Root River"), perhaps somewhere near present Peers. Not far from modern Edson they crossed to the north bank of the McLeod River and continued along this stream for three days, leaving it about the vicinity of Medicine Lodge, near where they were able to get their first clear view of the Rocky Mountains. From Edson westward, the trail followed quite closely the general route of modern Highway 16.

From Medicine Lodge the trail passed through a point close to Obed to strike the Athabasca River near Dalehurst. The Overlanders then turned southwestward along the south bank of the Athabasca, passing near Hinton to camp at the mouth of Prairie or Maskuta Creek (TM's "Prairie River"). It appears that the Overlanders then turned up Prairie Creek along the route of the present highway, although TM's statement that they followed the south bank of the Athabasca for four days after the time they first struck it casts some doubt on this assumption. In any case, they certainly camped in the Pocahontas area on the south bank of the Athabasca again, near Roche Miette, on 18 August.

The trail led onward from this point between Jasper and Talbot (TM's "White-fish") Lakes to the crossing place of the Athabasca a few miles north of modern Jasper. At Jasper they turned westward up the Miette River, which they were forced to wade through many times before reaching their 22 August camp on the north shore of Yellowhead Lake (TM's "Cow-dung Lake") west of the Continental Divide. From here the Overlanders had only to follow the Fraser River to reach Tête Jaune Cache, and this they did, passing over a rugged trail on the north shore of Moose Lake and continuing for three more days on the north side of the river.

At Tête Jaune Cache, as TM explains, the group divided. About ninety men, including TM, made rafts or canoes and embarked upon the

Fraser. The journey to Fort George was swift for those who met with no accidents in the river.

The remaining thirty-six Overlanders set out for the North Thompson River, intending to follow it to Thompson's River Post, also known as Fort Kamloops. Their path led up the valley of the Maclennan River, and for a day or two they had a relatively easy trail. After that they were forced to cut their way through heavy timber, making only eight to ten kilometres a day. From modern Valemount they crossed to the northern bend of the Canoe River and turned south up its tributary, Camp Creek. Passing over the height of land near modern Albreda, they proceeded down the river of the same name to its mouth on the North Thompson at the point where the Thompson, coming in from the west, makes a sharp turn to the south. Here they attempted to cut a trail directly to the Cariboo district up along the west fork but gave up after going about one and a half kilometres. (This trail was found and followed to its end the next year by Milton and Cheadle's guide, Louis Battenotte "the Assiniboine" [*North-west Passage by Land*, p. 274].) Returning to the river below the mouth of the Albreda, the Overlanders turned southward heading for Kamloops, cutting another short trail on the west side of the Thompson. In 1863 Milton and Cheadle also followed this trail and found it took them one-and-a-half days to reach its end. At some point which must have been just a few kilometres north of the modern railway marker at Thunder River, ninety-six kilometres by their trail from the Cache, the Overlanders gave up and stopped at a place they called "Slaughter Camp" to kill their cattle, dry the meat, and make rafts and canoes for river travel, after abandoning most of their horses.

There were two long sets of rapids on the river between "Slaughter Camp" and Kamloops. The first, called Murchison Rapids by Milton and Cheadle, ended just below Porte d'Enfer Canyon, which is shown on modern maps, and the second lay near the mouth of the Mad River. Some of the Overlanders' rafts and canoes were lost in accidents, and all had to be abandoned above the sections of roughest water. Some of the parties built new vessels and carried on, repeating the process more than once, for evidence from the HBC's Fort Kamloops Journal indicates that many of the men arrived on rafts, and not all on foot as TM suggests. Others may indeed have chosen to walk the last 175 to 190 kilometres on the "good trail" which led from Mad River to the fort. It is also possible that many who appeared at Kamloops on rafts had walked over part of the trail before deciding that the river was now safe for navigation. A revealing comparison shows that it took the Overlanders who descended the Fraser only eight days to get to Fort George, while the North Thompson River travellers needed forty to get from the Cache to Kamloops; the modern highway route to Kamloops is only seventy-two kilometres longer than that to Prince George. More details about the

1862 journey down the North Thompson River may be found in M.S. Wade's *Overlanders of '62; Cheadle's Journal of Trip across Canada 1862-1863;* Milton and Cheadle's *North-West Passage by Land;* and the Overlander De Witt's narrative, "Arrival of a Party of Overland Immigrants by the Head-waters of Thompson River" (*Colonist,* 3 November 1862).

For more specific, especially historical, information about the Overlanders' trail, see the separate short notes accompanying the present edition of TM's text.

Notes to the Introduction

*Full citations are provided for all sources not listed in the Selected Bibliography; all others are referred to by short title.

1. For a good discussion of earlier overland parties, see Wade's *Overlanders*.

   A guide by the name of James Sinclair led two parties of Métis people from Red River to Oregon overland through British territory, using Rocky Mountain passes in what is now southern British Columbia. The first party, in 1841, numbered about 130 people, and the second, in 1854, about 65 men, women, and children. These were apparently the only large groups, apart from the Overlanders of 1862, to make the crossing described. There is considerable confusion about exactly which pass or passes Sinclair used on his two journeys. Captain Blakiston of the 1858 Palliser expedition stated definitely that Sinclair used the Kananaskis or Lake River Pass in both 1841 and 1854 and that carts abandoned there and found by Blakiston belonged to the 1854 expedition. The pass now known as Sinclair Pass does not lie in the Rockies at all, but some distance to the west, "between the Brisco and Stanford Ranges, which separate the upper Kootenay from the upper Columbia" (Spry, *Palliser Papers*, p. lxxxiiin). Wade states that in 1841 Sinclair's party crossed by "either the Whiteman or Kananaskis Pass, and reached Colville one month later" than HBC Governor George Simpson on his whirlwind tour of that year. The consensus among historians today seems to be that in 1841 Sinclair probably used White Man Pass, and in 1854 Kananaskis (see ibid., pp. xlix, 641).

2. For full bibliographical information on TM's narrative see "A Note on the Text."

3. For full information on the other Overlander accounts, see the Bibliography.

4. The one account which is still generally available is Alexander's *Diary and Narrative*. Richard Alexander (1844-1915) was born in Edinburgh, Scotland, of James and Eliza Alexander, and he came to Canada with his parents in 1855. He was educated at the Model Grammar School and at Upper Canada College. He was to study medicine, but when his father returned to Scotland after his wife's death, Richard was forced to seek employment in business in Toronto.

   With W.G.R. Hind and other Torontonians, some of whom were friends, Alexander joined Stephen Redgrave's party in 1862. They travelled with the McMicking group on the *International* from Georgetown to Red River but did not leave Fort Garry until 10 June.

   After an arduous trip, Alexander arrived at Fort George on 8 October. With injured feet, and ill with influenza, he walked most of the way to Lillooet where he found work cutting wood for two days. Continuing on foot by the Harrison Lake route, he came across an issue of the *British Columbian* in which his "supposed" death by drowning was reported, together with a report of the actual deaths of his friends John Carpenter and Philip Leader. At New Westminster, John Robson lent Alexander five dollars and invited him to stay at his home.

During the next few years, Alexander worked as a miner at Cariboo, as a pack train attendant, and as a longshoreman at Victoria. In 1870 he became accountant for the Hastings Sawmill Company, rising to the post of manager in 1882. He was one of the founders of the city of Vancouver, serving on the incorporation committee, as alderman, on the school board, and on the board of health. He married in 1867, and he and his wife Emma Helen Tammadge had four children. For more information, see Alexander's *Diary and Narrative;* Alexander Papers, PABC; Wade, *Overlanders,* p. 158; Alexander's obituary, *Victoria Colonist,* 30 January 1915; Mrs. Richard Alexander's obituary, *Colonist,* 7 June 1916.

5. For general historical background on the British Columbia gold rushes, see Ormsby's *British Columbia,* Bancroft's *History of British Columbia,* Macfie's *Vancouver Island and British Columbia.*

6. James Douglas to Henry Labouchere, 6 April 1858, Vancouver Island, Governor, Correspondence Outward, Despatches to London, PABC.

7. See, for example, reports from the *Alta California,* 3 February; 5, 9, and 10 March; 12, 17, 19, 21, and 23 April 1858; and from the *Bulletin,* 3, 6, 14, and 19 April 1858.

8. Andrew F. Rolle, *California: A History,* 2d ed. (New York: Crowell, 1970), p. 224.

9. Caughey, *California Gold Rush,* p. 266.

10. Rolle, *California,* p. 315.

11. See the April reports from the *Alta California* cited above. An example of the kind of speculative reasoning that led to such rumours is found in one of the earliest works printed in Victoria, Alfred Waddington's *The Fraser Mines Vindicated, or the History of Four Months* (P. de Garro, 1858; repr., with an Introduction by W. Kaye Lamb [Vancouver: Robert R. Reid, 1949]), p. 44. Waddington mentions an estimate of $240,000 for the total California gold production in the first six months of mining in 1849, contrasted with a known production of $543,000 in B.C. for the period of June to October, 1858. These figures made it seem likely that B.C.'s gold production would outstrip California's. In fact, California's production for 1849 has been more reliably estimated at $20,000,000 to $30,000,000 (see Caughey, *California Gold Rush,* p. 171).

12. Macfie, *Vancouver Island and British Columbia,* p. 72. In a letter to Lytton, Douglas estimated the "supposed production" since June at 106,305 ounces, 40,000 ounces remaining in the hands of miners in the province (30 November 1858, Despatches to London, PABC).

13. Bancroft, *History of British Columbia,* p. 515n. Cariboo gold sold for an average of $16 per ounce at the time (ibid., p. 513n.).

14. The figure of fifteen hundred was governor Douglas's estimate (see ibid., p. 514n.).

15. Ibid., p. 482n.

16. A fascinating and now readily available map showing the early trails to the Cariboo district is the "Map of the Gold Regions in British Columbia, Compiled from Sketches and informations [*sic*] by His Excellency James Douglas, C.B. Governor of British Columbia and Vancouver Island,—and from data obtained from the most intelligent and reliable Miners, By Gust. Epner. (1862)," originally published by Britton and Co., San Francisco, and reprinted as the endpaper in Wade's *Cariboo Road.*

17. Alexander Leslie Fortune (1830-1915) was born at Huntingdon, Lower Canada, the eldest of three children of a Scots-born physician, Dr. Robert Fortune, and his wife Isabelle. He is said to have studied for the Presbyterian ministry as a young man, but to have been forced to give up this career because of poor health.

   In 1862 Fortune was a merchant at St. Anicet and had just married Bathia Ross when he decided to try his luck in Cariboo. He was the leader of the small group known as the Acton party and as such became a member of the committee which helped TM govern on the overland journey. With Joseph Robinson, A.L. Fortune took turns conducting the Sunday services on the trip. It has sometimes been claimed in popular histories of the Overlander trek that A.L. Fortune was one of those who travelled down the North Thompson River to Kamloops in September, 1862. In fact it was William Fortune (no relation), a young Englishman, who went down the Thompson. A.L. Fortune was one of those who rode the "Huntingdon" raft down the Fraser to Fort George. He was also one of the few Overlanders to visit the diggings in 1862. With James Wattie he walked to Williams Creek, leaving James's brother William at Quesnel. The two friends stayed at Richfield eight days but found no work, so they returned to Quesnel at the beginning of October, accompanied by Fortune's beloved Kildonan ox bought at Red River.

"We thought the road by Yale was very long for our ox's feet," Fortune wrote, "so we resolved to try the route from Alexander [Alexandria] to Bentick [Bentinck] Arm." Thus Fortune and the Wattie brothers were the only Overlanders to complete the journey by the Palmer or Barron pack trail, reaching the Pacific, as Alexander Mackenzie did, at Bella Coola. They had a rough, sometimes dangerous trip through territory where the smallpox epidemic and consequently the Chilcotin people's hostility against white men were at a height. After spending three weeks at Bella Coola, the Overlanders were taken by Indian canoe to Bella Bella and on to Fort Rupert at Beaver Harbour on Vancouver Island where they caught a steamer for Victoria.

At Victoria Fortune went into partnership with William Morrow, the Overlander who had twice been ·injured by his ox on the prairies. They opened the Overland Restaurant and boarding house on Broad Street near Fort Street in March, 1863. They gave this venture up in the spring of 1864, and Fortune walked from Yale to Williams Creek, prospecting there in the summers for two years and labouring on a farm at Lillooet in the winter. In 1866 he travelled to the Big Bend mines on the Columbia, and when floods drove

him out, he and Overlanders John Malcolm and Thomas Dunne, outfitted by Overlander John Mara from his store at Seymour Arm, began exploring and prospecting on Shuswap Lake 'down to Sicamous, through Mara Lake and down the Shuswap River into the Okanagan Valley.

HBC Governor Dallas had given the Overlanders good reports of the Okanagan in 1862. The men found these accurate and took up land six and a half kilometres north of present day Enderby. Malcolm's claim was taken over the next year by another Overlander, Mark Wallis, from Southwold, C.W., and, still later, Wallis turned it over to Fortune. He began farming in 1867, but for some years he also operated a freighting service, bringing supplies into the valley by canoe and scow along the route he had taken in 1866. His ranch prospered, and in 1874 he brought his wife to British Columbia.

In the early years Fortune was active in missionary work among the Indians in the north Okanagan Valley, and he acted as an intermediary between them and the settlers in 1877 when unrest among the Nez Percé in the U.S. spread across the border. Indeed, his racial and religious tolerance was remarkable for the time, and his compassion for the people, ravaged by alcohol and disease, was deep and consistent.

Fortune died in 1915, after having written in later years several short, lively accounts of his life and of the Overlander journey. His last house, still occupied, stands at a lovely spot on the bank of the Shuswap River south of Enderby. For more information, see Wade, *Overlanders;* Fortune's own "Collection"; "The Bentinck Arm Route" (*Colonist,* 3 January 1863); "Case Made for Historic Riverbank" (*Enderby Commoner,* 1 August 1975); Schubert, "Reminiscences"; G.D. Brown's introduction to Fortune's "Overlanders of 1862"; L. Norris, "An Argonaut of 1862," Okanagan Historical Society, *Sixth Report* (Vancouver: Wrigley, 1936; repr. Vernon, B.C.: *Vernon News,* 1970), pp. 263-77.

18. Fortune, "Collection," p. 17. The *Globe* items of 24 March and 2 April 1862 are reproduced in part in Wade, *Overlanders*, pp. 11, 46-47.

19. TM's figures in the present publication indicate that the largest group (from Queenston) contained only twenty-four men, but he is writing of those parties which followed him. The group organized by Stephen Redgrave at Toronto contained about forty-five. For more information about the different groups, see Wade, *Overlanders*, pp. 10-14.

20. Samuel Chubbuck (1837-1921) was TM's wife Laura's brother. He is said to have been a telegraph operator at Toronto and Detroit before 1862. According to M.S. Wade, he kept a diary of the overland journey which was lost in a fire in 1875 at Virginia City. Chubbuck left British Columbia in 1863 and later became a telegraph operator, postmaster, storekeeper, and finally a Wells Fargo agent in the United States. He died in Oakland, California (see Wade, *Overlanders*, pp. 166-67). For more information about Robert McMicking, see Appendix 1, "A Note on the McMicking Family."

21. Information on TM's family and early life has been derived from a wide range of sources: the McMicking family papers and other material described in Appendix 1, "A Note on the McMicking Family"; Robert McMicking Papers, PABC; Wade, *Overlanders*; Kerr, *Biographical Dictionary*, pp. 253-61; Victor G. Hopwood, "Thomas McMicking," *DCB* 7; Harkness, "Correspondence Outward"; Paul G. Cornell, "John Simpson," *DCB* 10:656; and from the following letters to the present editor: Kenneth Macpherson, Archives of Ontario, 31 March 1978; Sheila Moir, Presbyterian Church Committee on History, 25 April and 11 July 1978; R. Tapscott, Archives of Ontario, 6 June 1978; Linda Potter, Niagara-on-the-Lake Public Library, 31 October 1979; Deborah Rose, Niagara Historical Society, 24 April 1980; Inge Jahnke Saczkowski, Niagara Falls Public Library, 17 November 1979; Sheila Wilson, St. Catharines Public Library, 11 March 1980.

Reasons advanced for TM's narrow loss (by 95 votes) in the 1861 Niagara election include his sister Emma's claim that during the campaign he developed pneumonia, which "no doubt played a prominent part in his defeat." John Simpson was a well-known politician who had been mayor of Niagara for four years from 1852 and served as the Niagara representative in the provincial parliament from 1857. Simpson was re-elected in 1863, defeating Henry J. Boulton. Newspaper accounts of the 1861 campaign include "The Niagara Election," *St. Catharines Journal*, 20 June 1861; "Election Meeting," *The Niagara Mail*, 19 June 1861; "Election Intelligence," *St. Catharines Journal*, 11 July 1861.

22. Fortune, "Collection," p. 20.

23. Dr. Symington was an American who joined A.L. Fortune's Acton party in Minnesota. Near Breckenridge the group met a dying consumptive, named John Nichols or "Nicholas," who was returning by stage to the east. Symington "advised the sick man not to go back to friends nor doctors for he would surely die; but to come along with our overland party and if he died we would bury him. But the Doctor . . . had good hopes that the prairie air and the outdoor life might help to restore him." Nichols recovered as predicted. For this anecdote, which comprises all we know about Symington's personal history, see Fortune, "Collection," p. 23.

24. Nothing definite is known about the party led by Symington until it reached Edmonton. On 31 July 1862, the HBC Fort Edmonton Journal recorded the "Arrival of second party of miniors": "An other party of twenty miniors arived with wagons and thay have no oxen thay are to follow the others [i.e., McMicking's party]." On 1 August: "The miniors comenced crossing as thay are determined to follow the others, some of the party have lost thair oxen." On 6 August: "Weather fine the miniors left for St. Albert" (B.60/a/32, fos. 39d-40d). For more information, see Wade, *Overlanders*, pp. 130-32; McNaughton, *Overland to Cariboo*, pp. 103-13.

Margaret McNaughton relates that Dr. Symington was able to give the priest at Lac Ste Anne advice about the use of a box of homeopathic medicines which had been donated to the mission, and in his account Wade identifies the priest as Father Albert Lacombe. Lacombe was absent from the region on a journey to Fort Garry at the time, however, and did not return to Edmonton until 27 August 1862 (see note 27 on the Rennie party of Overlanders, below). E.O. Drouin, O.M.I., has identified the priest on duty at Lac Ste Anne as Fr. René Rémas, who may have received the advice mentioned from Symington, but Fr. Drouin notes that the story of Lacombe's getting information about the use of medicines may refer to a visit from "an itinerant Medic" (possibly Dr. James Hector, of Palliser's expedition) in 1858 (E.O. Drouin, Oblate Archives, to present editor, 10 May 1978). See also Katherine Hughes, *Father Lacombe: The Blackrobe Voyageur* (New York: Moffat, Yard and Co., 1911), pp. 79-80, 82-85; E.O. Drouin, *Lac Ste-Anne Sakahigan* (Edmonton: Editions de l'Hermitage, 1973); Milton and Cheadle, *North-West Passage by Land*, pp. 179-82; Wade, *Overlanders*, pp. 130-31.

25. Stephen Redgrave (1831-1903) was born in England, educated at Rugby, and married to a niece of the archbishop of Canterbury at the age of eighteen. Three years later the couple moved to Australia, where Redgrave served as a warden at a penal settlement and as a mounted policeman. According to his own account, he was wounded several times in gun battles with bushrangers. He also did some prospecting.

He arrived in Canada in 1859 after a short stay in South Africa and a visit home to England. In Toronto he became a sergeant with the city police, but resigned—according to one report, only a few hours before leaving on the train—to travel to B.C. with a group of about forty-five men he had helped organize. He seems to have been a restless, contradictory man who soon lost or willingly gave

up control of "his" party of miners after the departure from Fort Garry.

In B.C. he immediately went to work, as a number of the Overlanders did, labouring at roadbuilding; but by January 1863, he was again a policeman, first in Victoria and then in Williams Creek until 1865. Afterwards he mined for a time, but moved with his family, which eventually included six children, to a farm in Virginia in 1869. He returned to B.C. in 1873 and held several official positions: mining recorder and provincial constable for Cassiar (1876); sheriff for Kootenay (1884); Chinese collector and registrar of the County Court, Kootenay (1885); assessor and collector of revenue (1888). His wife died in 1893, and Redgrave married again the next year. The couple separated a few years later, and he died in 1903.

For further details, see Wade, *Overlanders*, pp. 158-59; Redgrave, "Journals"; Martha Lincoln Redgrave's obituary, *Golden Era*, 9 September 1893; Redgrave's obituary, *Vancouver Daily Province*, 26 March 1903; Vertical File, PABC, which gives references to numerous articles about Redgrave's activities and appointments in B.C. For a personal view of Redgrave's character, see Robert Harkness to his wife, on different occasions.

26. Love was an American from Kentucky, who, in 1858, with Minnesotan D.F. McLaurin and miners Thomas Clover and Alfred Perry, began a tour of the gold mines of California and B.C. The men ascended the Fraser River in 1860, prospecting on the way, and crossed the mountains through the Yellowhead Pass to Edmonton. During the winter they did some prospecting on the Saskatchewan and its tributaries. Love and McLaurin then proceeded to Red River and Minnesota for supplies.

McLaurin died the following winter, but Love was successful in publicizing what proved to be exaggerated estimates of the wealth of gold to be found in the Saskatchewan district. His enthusiasm and optimism inspired about ten of Redgrave's original party to choose him for their leader. In this position he was assisted by a guide named George Flett, and they travelled with some other Fort Garry men who had been planning to join Love and Flett before the arrival of the Canadians. Another group, presumably also composed of Fort Garry men and organized by John Whitford, joined forces with the Redgrave-Love-Flett party; and on 20 June, a few days after leaving Fort Garry, the whole company held a meeting at which "Whitford was voted to be guide and Whitford's and Love's party to lead alternately" (Alexander, *Diary and Narrative*, p. 9).

On 8 August 1862, the HBC Edmonton Journal reported the "Arival of a third party of Miniors [that is, after McMicking's and Symington's]: A party of sixty three men headed by Mrsrs Love and Flett arived some for Bow River some for this place some to go by the Jaspers house pass." The next day's entry states: "some of the party crossed thay go by Jaspers thay are as strong headed as the first and thay say that all that is told them is to deceave them." Journal entries for the next six days indicate that some of the Love-Flett party remained to prospect around Edmonton while others left for the Bow River on 12 August.

Milton and Cheadle met Love at Edmonton in 1863 and judged him to be more of a talker than a doer. His ultimate fate is uncertain. For more details, see the sources mentioned and the following: Wade, *Overlanders*, pp. 45-49; Hargrave, *Red River*, p. 61; Milton and Cheadle, *North-West Passage by Land*, p. 183; Cheadle, *Journal*, pp. 139-41.

John Whiteford or Whitford may be the man described by Peter Erasmus as "from Lac Ste. Anne, a Scotch half-breed whose nick-name was Ma-cheesk and whose given name was John Whitford," and who "enjoyed a reputation for leadership and was trusted for his judgement" among his own people and the Cree in a large area near Edmonton. Erasmus took part in a buffalo hunt in 1870 which was led by Whitford and later described Whitford's ac-

tions during the dramatic events of that hunt and of the smallpox epidemic that coincided with it (see Erasmus, *Buffalo Days and Nights*, pp. 201-9).

George Flett, "a Cree half-breed," according to Stephen Redgrave, was one of the "men fully competent to take charge" of an overland expedition to B.C. (*Toronto Globe*, 2 April 1862; quoted in Wade, *Overlanders*, p. 47).

H.Y. Hind stayed at the home of a "George Flett," probably the same man, at a farm on the banks of the Assiniboine, some twenty-five kilometres west of Fort Garry, on 15 September 1857 (Hind, *Exploring Expeditions*, 1:148).

27. The Rennie brothers and their friends were long incorrectly thought to have been members of the three earlier Overlander parties who chose to linger at Edmonton to do some prospecting, then were caught by winter when they tried to reach Fort George late in the year. Milton and Cheadle give an incomplete version of the ensuing tragic events in *North-West Passage by Land*, pp. 321-23 (and Bruce Hutchison alludes to the incident in passing in *The Fraser* [Toronto: Rinehart, 1950], p. 105).

The full story is to be found in contemporary newspaper accounts. The first is in the form of a letter in the *British Columbian*, 11 July 1863. The writers were William and Gilbert Rennie, two of the men in the party. Their companions were John Helstone, John R. Wright, and Thomas McG. Rennie, brother of the authors. All were from London, C.W., which they had left on 15 May 1862.

After travelling overland from St. Paul to Red River, the five left Fort Garry on 8 July "in company with Pere Le'Comte [*sic*—undoubtedly Father Lacombe, who did make a journey from Red River to Edmonton about this time] R.C. Priest of Lake St. Ann, and party." On 27 August they reached Edmonton, where they left Lacombe, and on 24 September they arrived at Jasper, where they obtained a guide to Tête Jaune Cache. At the Cache they "gave a horse for one canoe and made another" and killed and dried the meat from four oxen. On 17 October they launched the lashed-together canoes, but they made slow progress down river.

About 160 kilometres above Fort George, on 30 October, the large canoe got stuck on a submerged rock. After three days and two nights in a storm and without fire, three of the men tried to run the rapids of the ice-filled river in the small canoe, which immediately capsized. Wright was carried a mile and a half downstream but made shore; the others got back to the rock. Next day a line was sent ashore to Wright and he pulled the other four over; but by this time all except William and Gilbert Rennie had frozen hands and eet. A conference was held, and it was decided that the latter two should try to make Fort George, thought to be only sixty-five kilometres away.

Twenty-eight days later, starving and by now also with frozen limbs, the Rennies were taken in at the fort, where they spent fifty-three days convalescing. Two Indians made an attempt to reach the stranded men, but returned after a few hours, saying the snow was too deep and the river only partly frozen. While at Fort George, the Rennies "were requested several times by Mr. Charles [HBC agent in charge] to leave and go to the Mouth of the Quesnelle as he was getting short of provisions," but they were too ill to depart until 26 January 1863.

On reaching Quesnel, the Rennies finally received news of their companions:

Early in the spring (the word was brought down by Mr. Ogden) the Indians from Fort George went up to the camp and found the bones of one outside the tent and the other two wrapped up in the blankets, dead. . . . From the time we left our companions until we reached· the Mouth of Quesnelle, we camped out 35 nights in extremely cold weather with only one blanket between us. We are now on our way to

Victoria. We are, Sir, yours respectfully, William Rennie, Gilbert Rennie, Survivors of the Company.

The *Colonist* had actually given an earlier version of the story in March. The victims' names were not known at the time, but the paper severely censured Thomas Charles for trying to force the survivors to leave for Quesnel before they were fully recovered and for not persuading the Indians to make more of an effort to reach the stranded party (see "Man's Inhumanity to Man," 21 March 1863, and "Men Left behind on the Fraser," 25 March and 6 April 1863).

The sensational sequel to this story was reported by John Giscome, a Jamaican prospector who had spent the winter of 1862-63 in a cabin near Fort George. Giscome said that news had reached the fort in March that natives who came upon the Canadians' camp had actually found two men still alive and that these had murdered the third and were eating him. They had driven the Indians away with pistols.

Thomas Charles asked Giscome to examine the camp, which the prospector would pass on a planned trip up-river. Giscome had to bribe his guide to take him to the place, and when they got there they discovered clear evidence of cannibalism on two of the bodies. Giscome did not see the third man; but he was later told by an Indian companion that his body lay about 350 metres away in the bush and that he had been murdered, possibly by Indians who had then plundered the camp. Giscome concluded that the men had lived for about ten weeks, had killed and eaten one another, and that the third man had been murdered by Indians ("A Fearful Tragedy," *Colonist*, 14 December 1863). An article of the same title published in the *British Columbian*, 23 December 1863, vehemently attacked Giscome's conclusions, suggesting instead (without explaining the evidence of cannibalism, which the tribes of the region found horrifying) that Indians had murdered all three men. For more information, see the sources mentioned and Morice, *Northern Interior*, pp. 300-302.

28. Hind, *Sketch of an Overland Route*, pp. 10-14. For more details on the carts and trail used by the Overlanders, see Appendix 2, "A Note on the Trail."

29. George Wallace (?-1887) had a colourful career after 1862, but almost nothing is known of him before that time. The information that he was connected with the *Globe* comes from Wade, *Overlanders*, p. 12. The record of Wallace's activities in B.C. confirms that he did know something of the newspaper business, for in November, 1862, he advertised the establishment of "The Globe, New Weekly Paper, to be published in Victoria" (*Colonist*, 10 November 1862). But the paper either never appeared or had only a very short run, for no other trace of it has surfaced. It seems Wallace then joined the staff of the *Colonist* as a reporter, but he again ventured into publishing in April, 1863, in partnership with C.W. Allen, with the debut of the *Victoria Daily Evening Express*. The *Express* went out of business in February, 1865; but by June of that year Wallace had established the *Cariboo Sentinel* at Barkerville, after buying the handprinting press first brought to B.C. by Bishop Demers and once used by the *Colonist*. Wallace sold the *Sentinel* early in 1866, and in April of that year the first issue of his third (or, indeed, perhaps fourth) B.C. newspaper, the *British Columbia Tribune*, appeared at Yale.

Wallace had a reputation for publishing stories which were somewhat racier than those carried by the established papers, the *Colonist* at Victoria and the *British Columbian* at New Westminster. John Robson, editor of the latter, violently attacked Wallace in an editorial of 25 April 1866, occasioned by the appearance of the *Tribune*. He deplored what he called Wallace's "insane ravings" and "style of coarsest scurrility" and expressed the hope that these would never be found in the new paper. Wallace also made headlines in Victoria while editor of the *Sentinel* for physically attacking one of the owners of the *Colonist* because of some unknown insult Wallace considered had been offered him in print.

The *Tribune* was closed for the season in October, 1866, shortly after Wallace was elected to the Legislative Council for the district of Yale. Wallace resigned the office in January, 1867, and left for New York and England, already wealthy. According to a report in the *Colonist*, 26 June 1867, he had "cleared a large fortune by a fortunate speculation in Japan." Yet there remains considerable mystery about Wallace's business activities and the source of his wealth, which seems, in fact, to have been very great at one time. His obituary in the *Colonist*, 19 May 1887, reveals that he had cleared half a million dollars by exhibiting and managing a troupe of Japanese jugglers on a tour of the U.S. and Europe. He then lost his money through the failure of a British banking house, but he recouped some of his losses by managing the famous Siamese twins on a grand European tour in 1870.

Later Wallace returned to Montreal, married, and became a correspondent for several North American newspapers. But his wife died in 1883, and he apparently never recovered from the loss. The couple had two small sons at the time. Wallace died less than five years later.

For more information, see the newspaper articles mentioned and the following: James Nesbitt, "Japanese Jugglers Made Victorian Rich," *Colonist*, 2 December 1956, magazine section; Vertical File, PABC; Irving and Amy Wallace, *The Two* (New York: Bantam, 1979), pp. 314-15, 320-21, 328.

30. As noted, the details of the meeting at Long Lake are drawn from a number of Overlander accounts. A.L. Fortune, with his usual original turn of phrase, described the appearance of the caravan as "not picturesque" but "primitive galore" ("Collection," p. 28).

31. Alexander Grant Dallas (1818?-82), born in Scotland, had engaged in trade at Shanghai before being

appointed president of the council and company representative of the Western Department of the HBC at Victoria in the late 1850's. He succeeded James Douglas, who became governor of the two colonies of Vancouver Island and British Columbia. Dallas married Douglas's daughter Jane and once sued his father-in-law in his capacity as HBC representative, claiming certain land for the company which Douglas claimed for the government. While at Victoria, Dallas was involved in the start of the famous "Pig War" which resulted in the joint occupation of San Juan Island by British and American troops in 1860 (see Begg, *History of British Columbia*, pp. 248-62. Dallas invested much of his wealth, accumulated in the Far East, in the HBC. In 1861 he succeeded George Simpson as governor of Rupert's Land.

British Columbians may be interested in Dallas's assessment of the type of immigrant needed for the colony of Vancouver Island in 1862:

> It [the colony] is not the country for broken-down gentlemen or "swells." Washing costs 72 cents per dozen. You cannot get your boots brushed under a shilling; servants' wages are five to eight pounds per month. This is enough to dismay a professional man with a family, but it is good news for the washerwoman, the shoe-black and the servant of all work. Single men can generally rough it out, and the restaurants, generally kept by Frenchmen, are far better than they are in London.
>
> Permit me to draw attention to a crying evil—the want of women. I believe there is not one to every one hundred men at the mines; without them the male population will never settle in this country, and innumerable evils are the consequence. A large number of the weaker sex could obtain immediate employment as domestic servants, at high rates of wages, with the certainty of marriage in the background.

> The miner is not very particular—"plain, fat, and 50" even would not be objected to; while good looking girls would be the nuggets and prized accordingly. An immigration of such character would be a great boon to the colony as I am sure it would be to many under-paid and over-worked women who drag out a weary existence in the dismal streets and alleys of this metropolis (*London Times*, 1 January 1862).

Dallas spoke eloquently of the beauty and fertility of the Okanagan valley, and his praise inspired Alexander Fortune to investigate the region and eventually settle there:

> Gov. Dallas had been in many places before he visited British Columbia, and he did not say much about this province to raise our esteem of it except that part known as the Okanagan valley. He declared that this was the most charming piece of country he had ever seen, what with the mountains, timber, rocks, charming lakes and creeks. The bold mountain slopes and benches covered with grass and bloom of flowers and the wide plains and vallies filled with grass, and game so plentiful, birds in great flocks and deer in large herds. He thought it a veritable paradise fit to be a Heaven for the pure of heart and the lover of nature and natures creator ("Collection," p. 26-27).

For further information on Dallas, see Wade, *Overlanders*, pp. 170-71; Wallace, *Macmillan DCB*, p. 170; Rich, *History of the Hudson's Bay Company*, 2:812, 873; James Nesbitt, "Old Homes and Families," *Colonist*, 26 November 1950, magazine section; Shirlee Smith, HBCA, to the present editor, 15 February 1980.

32. Robert McMicking, "Journal," p. 4.
33. Fortune, "Collection," pp. 26-27.
34. Caughey, *California Gold Rush*, p. 106.
35. Fortune, "Collection," pp. 62-63.
36. Caughey, *California Gold Rush*, p. 106.
37. M.S. Wade is the source for the little

that is known about John Sellar and
his older brother William, who was
also an Overlander. They were the
"sons of Joseph Sellar, an Englishman, and his wife Letitia, an Irish-
woman. They did not remain long in
B.C., but drifted into the U.S. and
returned to Huntingdon in 1870.
John . . . being left some means by an
uncle, went into business in Toronto
as a boot and shoe dealer. Later he
sold the business and went to Dakota,
where he took up farming and
married. Then moved to Minne-
apolis . . . where he and his wife
died" (*Overlanders*, p. 159).

According to the evidence in his
own long journal of the trek, John
was impatient and sarcastic. For him,
the funniest moments of the journey
occurred when others got into
difficulties which made them look a
little ridiculous. He did, however,
possess the merit of being industrious and energetic. William was
popular and responsible, earning
praise from A.L. Fortune for his
piloting of the big "Huntingdon"
raft, of which he was elected captain,
on the Fraser River.

For more information, see Sellar,
"Journal."

38. Alexander Fortune described how
this problem surfaced right at the
beginning of the journey, when
many of those who had got to White
Horse Plain early, including Sellar,
pushed on with the single guide,
leaving the others to follow next day
unaided. Fortune wrote that "we got
out of bed next morning early and
resolved that no cart nor ox should
move until the balance of the
company would make up to us. Some
of us made it publicly known that the
first man that would start before they
got orders from the Captains would
have his ox shot before him"
("Collection," p. 28). This threat
worked for a time, but later, as the
notes in Sellar's diary suggest, the
group was apparently allowed to
start early quite consistently, as long
as they did not take the guide with
them. See his "Journal," pp. 33-35,
where he makes several references to
how the group "started leaving half
[the] party behind," and pp. 39-40,

where he tells how they crossed the
Qu'Appelle to camp for Sunday
"leaving most all the remainder of
the Company at Fort Ellice. There we
togather split off from the main
boddy, & travelled ahead the cause of
the split being the delay of certain
Parites, who knew Nothing about
Carts & Cattle or anything else save
standing & looking at others working, or getting behind a Counter
neither of which will be of any benifit
to a man when his Ox & Cart is stuck
fast in a mud hole."

39. Ibid., p. 29.
40. Catherine Schubert (23 April 1835-18
July 1918) emigrated to the U.S. with
her brother from her home at
Ballybrick, near Rathfriland, County
Down, Ireland, during or shortly
after the famine years of 1847-49. In
Massachusetts in 1856 she married
Augustus Schubert (4 March 1827-10
July 1908), a native of Dresden,
Saxony. The couple soon moved west
to St. Paul, where they "kept a beer-
hall." Fear of Indian troubles there
caused them to move on to Fort
Garry, across the international boun-
dary, in December, 1860.

Mrs. Schubert seems to have been a
cheerful, adventurous woman, who
was moved by the beauty of the
Rocky Mountains and wept bitterly
when forced to abandon her "good
old horse, the buckskin" which had
carried her, with two of her children
in baskets at the sides of her saddle,
from Edmonton as far as the North
Thompson River (Schubert, "Reminiscences," p. 8).

The worst part of the journey
followed. McMicking, who relates
this part of Mrs. Schubert's story
from the sketchy verbal accounts of a
few of her companions, captures
some of the horrors of the trail from
Tête Jaune Cache to Kamloops. He
does not stress the telling fact that it
took the Schuberts six weeks to get
down the Thompson, whereas the
men on the Fraser arrived at Fort
George only ten days after leaving the
Cache.

Mrs. Schubert gave birth to a
healthy daughter, named Rose, only
hours after the family arrived, ragged
and starving, at Kamloops on 14

October 1862. This child was one of the first white babies born in the Kamloops district. There is a famous story that an Indian woman attended Mrs. Schubert, and carried the child outside the tent when it was born, exclaiming "It is Cumloops, Cumloops," and that the parents considered naming the baby "Kamloops" (see Schubert, "Reminiscences," p. 10). However, Mrs. Agnes Shiell LeDuc, wife of Rose's son Frederick, stated in conversation with the present editor that this story was a legend she had heard Catherine Schubert deny. Instead, Mrs. LeDuc claimed, when Augustus Schubert visited the Indian dwellings nearby to ask for help, the women there misunderstood and refused to come with him. He had to help his wife deliver the baby alone, after which news travelled back to the Indian village and women came to help care for mother and daughter.

The baby was born on the opposite side of the North Thompson River from the post, and the HBC "Fort Kamaloops Journal" for 1862, kept by clerk William Manson, does not mention "Shoeburt" until 8 November. The family wintered in Kamloops, living in one of the buildings of the old fort, while Augustus worked for the HBC as carpenter and cook. The Schuberts then moved to Lillooet, and later to Clinton, though Augustus spent his summers mining in the Cariboo for about fifteen years after 1863. Mrs. Schubert became matron at the Cache Creek Boarding School in 1877, where she taught "domestic science" for six years. Her husband took up land at Spallumcheen in the North Okanagan Valley in that year, and the family moved there in 1883. The Schuberts had six children, including the three who accompanied their parents on the overland journey: Augustus, born in 1857; Mary Jane, born about 1858; and James, born 1860.

For more details, see the sources cited and the following: Wade, *Overlanders*, pp. 171-72; "E.M.C." (Mrs. E.M. Clarke), "Rathfriland Heroine," *The Outlook* (Rathfri-

land, Northern Ireland), 19 and 26 February 1976. For Schubert family obituaries see: Augustus, Sr., *Armstrong Advertiser*, 30 July 1908; Catherine, *Armstrong Advertiser*, 25 July 1918; James, *Similkameen Star*, 17 March 1938; Rose Schubert Swanson, *Armstrong Advertiser*, 11 January 1942, and *Vancouver Sun*, 16 January 1942; Augustus, Jr., *Armstrong Advertiser*, 14 November 1946.

41. Fortune, "Collection," p. 31.
42. Ibid., p. 64.
43. The following comes from Robert Harkness to his wife Sabrina, n.d. (probably written in late 1862 from New Westminster):

> McMicking is one of the finest men I ever saw, well educated and intelligent, but like myself he was unfortunate in business and in much the same way. He was a candidate for the representation of Niagara last election but was defeated by Simpson after a close election. He is now here, like myself now making shingles, & yet again like myself he has left a wife and three little ones about like ours in Canada. He has written an account of our trip which is now being published in the British Columbian newspaper. I am saving the papers to take home.

44. "Rochette" may be Charles Racette, a Red River Métis who was one of about fourteen men hired by Captain John Palliser in 1857 for his expedition's first season's work on the plains. Racette was again engaged by Palliser in 1858, and he accompanied Captain Blakiston in his exploration of the Kootenay and Boundary passes that year (see Spry, *Palliser Papers*, p. 557). Racette seems to have given good service and would have gained an unusual knowledge of the western plains and the mountains, two facts which would have been a great recommendation to Taché when he was asked to help find a guide for the Overlanders. On the other hand, Margaret McNaughton—whose evidence, however, is often unreliable—wrote of Rochette: "The party afterwards

discovered that this was the third time this guide had performed the same trick. While at Fort Garry it was told them that Rochette was a bad character, but as he was so highly recommended by Bishop Tache, they thought he had either been slandered or that the parties who decried him were mistaken in the man" (*Overland to Cariboo*, pp. 44-45).

45. Alexandre Antonin Taché (1823-94), born at Rivière du Loup, L.C., of a well-known family, was educated at Montreal. In 1844 he became a novice of the Order of Oblates of Mary Immaculate. He was sent as a missionary to Red River in 1845, and rising swiftly, he was appointed second bishop of St. Boniface on the death of Bishop Provencher, and archbishop and metropolitan in 1871. From 1853 he sat on the Council of Assiniboia. In 1870 he was called back from Rome to announce an amnesty for the rebels at Red River, and he was influential in restoring peace. Taché also took part in early negotiations over the Manitoba schools question. He wrote numerous short histories of his life before his death in Winnipeg.

A.L. Fortune singled out Taché for special praise for his help: "We found his Lordship kind, ready to give us much information about the Lone land and the Indian tribes while he was with us on the steamer. And he was frequently troubled by us for information while our party was preparing for our journey over the plains" ("Collection," pp. 25-26).

During Taché's career the Catholic Church became strong in the Northwest. For more information, see Rich, *History of the Hudson's Bay Company*, 1:897-98, 901, 938, 932-34; Morton, *History of the Canadian West to 1870-71*, pp. 870-71, 910-11; Wallace, *Macmillan DCB*, p. 732.

46. One case in point was described by Alexander Fortune, as outlined in note 38 above. Another incident occurred a few days later among TM's party (see Fortune, "Collection," p. 30). A third such happening, which had serious consequences and almost ended in tragedy when

the men left behind ran out of food, occurred with a different guide and some of the Redgrave party in the Rocky Mountains (see Alexander, *Diary and Narrative*, pp. 20-22).

47. Information about TM's career at New Westminster is derived from the following sources: Archibald Thompson to his family, quoted in Wade, *Overlanders*, p. 118; McMicking family papers described in Appendix 1, "A Note on the McMicking Family"; Margaret McDonald, "New Westminster" (M.A. thesis, University of British Columbia, 1947), pp. 304, 359; Harkness Papers, PABC; *New Westminster British Columbian*, 15 April and 7 November, 1863, 2 July 1864, 15 February 1865, 21 February, 21 April, 20 June, 29 August, and 5 September 1866; *Victoria Colonist*, 20 January 1865, 28 and 31 August 1866.

48. The Hyack Fire Company, a volunteer unit, was organized in 1861. The name is from a Chinook jargon word meaning "fast, swift, or hurry," and so a free translation yields "Hurry-up Fire Company."

New Westminster still celebrates a "Hyack Festival" annually in May. The festival had its start when the men of the Hyack Fire Company organized a parade on Victoria Day. Until 1870 the 21-gun salute fired on that day was performed in the conventional manner, using a cannon. When the cannon broke down, former members of the Royal Engineers improvised a salute using gunpowder placed between two blacksmith's anvils and ignited by means of a hot poker. The same anvils have been fired every year since 1871. The fourteen members of the Honorable Hyack Anvil Battery wear red and black uniforms and must be native sons of New Westminster. For more information, see "Hyack Battery," Vertical File, New Westminster Public Library.

49. The *British Columbian*, 21 April 1866, reported that "a more popular appointment could not have been made, and we feel assured that Mr. McMicking, whose office will not always be of the most agreeable

character, while he will execute judgment with firmness, will not, by the exercise of arbitrary authority, render himself unnecessarily offensive to parties with whom, in the discharge of his duties, he may be brought into contact."

50. This distance below the city of New Westminster would put the location of the accident in the vicinity of today's South Vancouver district, possibly near Twigg or Mitchell Island. The *British Columbian*, 29 August 1866, reported that friends near whose home the mishap had occurred were named Miller and that the "Governor's steam yacht also went down to aid in the search for the bodies, and returned about 11 o'clock at night, bringing home the surviving members of the family. A few hours later the body of Mr. McMicking was raised and brought to town." Frank's body was never found.

51. John Andrew Mara was born at Toronto, 21 July 1840, the first son of John and Annie Mara. He was educated in Toronto and apparently worked in business there, possibly as a clerk, before joining Redgrave's party in 1862. He left this group to join TM's at Fort Garry.

In 1874 Mara bought the HBC steamer *Marten*, and it became the nucleus of his steamboat company. His eventual monopoly of trade and supply systems, augmented by his political power, made him a formidable economic rival of the HBC at Kamloops when John Tait was in charge in the 1870's; and Tait is alleged to have considered Mara ruthless in his business methods.

In 1882 Mara married Alice, sister of the Honourable G.H. Barnard and of the later Lieutenant-Governor Frank S. Barnard and daughter of F.J. Barnard, M.P., founder of the B.C. Express Company. The couple had two children, and their home was the grandest in Kamloops.

Around 1890-92 Mara, with F.S. Barnard, Forbes Vernon, Moses Lumby, and others, became a chief shareholder in the Shuswap and Okanagan Railway Co. The line ran south from Sicamous along Mara Lake, and the first station was built at the tiny community of Mara. After moving to Victoria in 1898, Mara continued his business activities, acting as director of several mining companies. For more information, see Mara's obituary, *Colonist*, 12 February 1920; James Nesbitt, "Old Homes and Families"; Balf, *Kamloops*.

52. John Fannin (1837-1904) was born in Kemptville, where he taught school. He is said to have once struck one of his pupils so hard with an oak ruler that she lost consciousness, but the child's daughter, relating the story many years later, wrote that her mother "bore him no grudge." When Fannin was older he was reputed to have been a favourite with children. Fannin was a member of the Queenston party of Overlanders and travelled with TM as far as Tête Jaune Cache, but there he chose to throw in his lot with the group which travelled down the North Thompson to Kamloops.

Fannin played the cornet well, so undoubtedly he was one of those Overlanders who gave concerts on the prairies, as a member of a "Musical Association." He also composed songs, one of which was published in the *Colonist* later. According to Wade, Fannin also "conducted a short-lived humorous journal, *The Comet*," in British Columbia.

After his appointment to the Provincial Museum, he organized the Natural History Society at Victoria and led many field trips to collect specimens and make observations for the museum. A lake, creek, and some mountains near Burrard Inlet were named after Fannin in 1928. Fannin never married.

For more information see Wade, *Overlanders*, p. 166; Dorothy Blakey Smith, memo, Vertical File, PABC; Annie Grahame, "John Fannin, Naturalist: An Appreciation," *Colonist*, 26 June 1904; Mrs. F.H. Anderson to the editor of the *Colonist*, 22 August 1966; Fannin's obituary, *Colonist*, 21 June 1904.

53. William Fortune (1835-1914), a young Yorkshireman who had emigrated to Canada in 1857, settled near

Kamloops where he arrived after rafting and walking down the North Thompson and later became one of that district's most substantial citizens. The HBC hired him in October, 1862, to work on the new fort then being built on the south side of the river, and he continued in the company's employ for seven years.

He bought land at Tranquille and started a flour mill and a sawmill. In 1877-78 he had built for him at Tranquille the *Lady Dufferin*, first sidewheeler in the district, for freighting and passenger traffic on the lakes and rivers between Savona and Spallumcheen. Finally he turned his attention to fruit-farming and ranching, and in 1907, when he retired, he sold his property to the government for a sanatorium for tuberculosis patients.

His wife Jane McWha Fortune, or "Lady Jane," was renowned for her excellent cooking and her business abilities and also for her determination and boldness when she felt herself wronged. She is reported to have thrown no less a personage than John Mara off the steamer into the lake, chased another young man into the water, and boxed the ears of an Indian who refused to pay what she asked for some flour.

For more information on William and Jane Fortune, see Balf, *Kamloops*, p. 45; Fort Kamloops Journal for October-November, 1862; Wade, *Overlanders*, p. 161; William Fortune's obituary, *Kamloops Inland Sentinel*, 1 December 1914; Jane Fortune's obituary, *Kamloops Standard-Sentinel*, 26 April 1918.

54. John Bowron (1837-1906) was born at Huntingdon, L.C., the son of a Yorkshire-born lumber-mill owner who "during [the] war of 1812 supplied British troops in Canada with beef" (Wade, *Overlanders*, p. 168). John Bowron was educated at Huntingdon Academy and studied law before setting out on the overland trek in 1862 in company with his cousin, W.B. Schuyler, and his friend G.C. Tunstall. Bowron settled in the Cariboo district in 1863. He was a founder of the Cariboo Literary Institute and Lending Library and postmaster at Camerontown (later Barkerville) in addition to the official posts mentioned. He married twice. With his first wife, Emily P. Edwards, whom he married in 1869, he had four children, and with his second wife, Elizabeth Watson, whom he married in 1897, he had one daughter.

For more information, see Wade, *Overlanders*; Vertical File, PABC; Emily Bowron's obituary, *Colonist*, 6 June 1895; John Bowron's obituary, *Colonist*, 7 September 1906.

55. George Christie Tunstall (1836-1911) was born at Montreal, son of James and Elizabeth Tunstall. He was educated at Sorel and at Lower Canada College. He mined in Cariboo for a time, then was appointed government agent at Kamloops (1879), gold commissioner at Granite Creek (1885), registrar of the county court for the district of Yale (1886), gold commissioner at Revelstoke (1890), and gold commissioner and government agent at Kamloops again. He married Annie Morgan, with whom he had two sons. An interesting footnote to Tunstall's career is that he succeeded John Ussher, murdered by the McLean brothers and Alex Hare in a famous crime in 1879, as government agent at Kamloops (see Balf, *Kamloops*, p. 74). For more information see Wade, *Overlanders*, p. 169; Tunstall's obituary, *Colonist*, 9 January 1911.

56. Little is known about Arthur Robertson. He was the son of the jailkeeper at Goderich, Canada West, and had been educated as a civil engineer (see Wade, *Overlanders*, p. 169; Dobson Prest to father, December 1862).

Notes to William G.R. Hind

1. Unless otherwise indicated in the text or notes, the details of Hind's life are taken from Harper, *Hind*.
2. A drawing entitled "Panama May 1863" and signed "W.H.T. Ellis" appears at the end of Hind's sketchbook. It shows a small city nestled in mountains at the edge of the water and is in a style quite different from that of the other sketches.
3. Alexander, *Diary and Narrative*, p. 12.
4. From Hind's obituary in the *King's County Record* (Sussex, N.B.), 22 November 1889, quoted in Harper, *Hind*, p. 26.
5. See Robert Harkness to his wife, from Edmonton, 23 July 1862, and letter fragment, n.d.
6. Fortune, "Collection," p. 37.
7. Alexander, *Diary and Narrative*, p. 15.
8. "The Huntingdon party who had preceded us made it better for us in getting over these fallen trees—poor fellows theirs was a task indeed.... too much praise cannot be given to these hardy young men and I frankly admit that had we not such good p[e]rsevering industrious young fellows ahead of us ... we should never have got thro" (Redgrave, "Journals," pp. 279-80).
9. Alexander, *Diary and Narrative*, p. 21.
10. Virtually nothing is known of the circumstances surrounding Phillip Leader's death (see Wade, *Overlanders*, p. 135). McMicking states he was from Huron County; Wade, that he was of the Goderich party. The report of his and Carpenter's death in the *British Columbian*, 25 October 1862, entitled "One Man Drowned, and Five More Supposed to Be," identified Leader as "of Saugeen, C.W."
11. Alexander, *Diary and Narrative*, p. 30.
12. Richard Henry Alexander, "Diary." The typescript actually reads "Hurd" instead of "Hind," but the original shows "Hind."
13. J.R. Harper to present editor, 6 May 1977.
14. Sellar, "Journal," pp. 73-74.
15. Kenneth Saltmarche, Introduction to Harper, *William G.R. Hind* (Windsor: Willistead Art Gallery, 1967), p. 3.

Notes to the Text

1. A summary of what is known about the men in the Queenston party follows. The information is derived from the text and biographical notes in Wade's *Overlanders*, from the sources indicated in the card index of pre-1900 British Columbia newspapers in the Provincial Archives of British Columbia in Victoria, and from specific sources mentioned.

   Archibald Thompson (1830-1909) was one of those Overlanders who travelled down the North Thompson River from Tête Jaune Cache to Kamloops. A widower, he remained in British Columbia for about two years, working in the Cariboo mines with John Fannin and later resuming his trade as a blacksmith at Victoria. He then moved to California and later to Michigan, and eventually he retired to Stamford, Ontario, where he died. Dr. Wade used some of Thompson's letters in writing his history of the trek, but they have since disappeared. For more information, see Robert Harkness to his wife Sabrina, 1862 to 1865; Dobson Prest to different members of his family, 1862 and 1863.

   John Boland, who according to Robert Harkness was the treasurer of the Queenston party, returned to Ontario in the spring of 1863, went into business at Queenston, and later moved to Denver, Colorado. James Willox was one of the two men who narrowly escaped drowning in the McLeod River, see text, p. 34, and note 66. Leonard Crysler (1836-85) was a youth with some artistic ability

who stayed only a few months in B.C. Later he became a physician but never practised. Joseph Robinson (1822-1911) emigrated from England to Canada about 1849. After the overland journey, he returned to the east early in 1863 and resumed farming.

   Copies of affectionate letters from Robert Harkness (1833-84) to his young wife and family survive in PABC. They provide information about the 1862 journey and reveal Harkness's homesickness and poverty while he laboured at odd jobs and in the Cariboo mines trying to save enough money to return home. He had been a merchant in Iroquois before joining the Overlanders. While he was away, Sabrina taught school to support their three children, and when he returned he took her place. Later he ventured into innkeeping and finally became a newspaperman, buying the *Picton Times*. His son Robert was one of the founders of the *Daily News*, Vancouver's first daily newspaper. For more information, see Harkness letters; copy of Mary Dell Harkness Race to her daughter Isabel Kathleen Race Eddy, c. 1952, Harkness Papers, PABC.

   I.D. Putnam was another of those Overlanders who travelled by the North Thompson route to Fort Kamloops. James Rose left B.C. early and settled in Berkeley, California, where his son-in-law later became mayor. William Gilbert was the other Overlander who was nearly drowned crossing the McLeod River;

he lived to return to Ontario in 1863.

Dobson Prest (?-1885), a relative by marriage of Thomas McMicking, stayed throughout 1863 and possibly for some time after that in B.C., working at roadbuilding and as a carpenter at Victoria. He then moved to the U.S. and died in California. Copies of some of his letters written in 1862 and 1863 to his family in the east survive in PABC. They provide a number of interesting details about the expedition and the Overlanders' experiences in B.C. through 1863. For example, Prest reported that Catherine Schubert did his washing on the journey, in addition to all her other duties caring for her family.

John Hunniford, a young Irishman, left his wife and three small children in St. Catharines in 1862. He kept a laconic diary in which he recorded his increasingly doleful impressions of the journey. Upon arriving in B.C., he travelled down to Victoria, where he worked on the Craigflower Road. In late 1863 he returned home, where he became a successful merchant. For more information, see Hunniford, "Journal."

Simeon Cumner left B.C. in 1863 and moved to the U.S., where he died soon after of exposure in the California mountains. For information about Samuel Chubbuck, TM's brother-in-law, see introduction note 20. W.H.G. Thompson, "Lieutenant" of the Queenston party, was one of the Overlanders still living in B.C. in 1889 (Begg, *History of British Columbia*, p. 447). He was probably the William Henry Guelph Thompson elected to the board at a "Hospital Meeting at Barkerville" reported by the *Cariboo Sentinel*, 5 June 1875. For more information about William Fortune, see introduction note 53.

Peter Marlow (1830-1912) was a successful farmer near Queenston in 1862. He and his wife sold all their possessions before Marlow left for B.C. He laboured at a sawmill on the coast after doing a little mining in B.C., but he returned to Ontario in 1865 and resumed farming. He died at Grimsby.

2. The *Frank Steele* was a sidewheeler built at Cincinnati, Ohio, and dismantled at La Crosse, Wisconsin. It was in operation from 1857 to 1864, and was a packet of 122 tonnes, 53 metres in length and 8.5 metres wide, with a wooden hull and a texas deck. The steamboat ran in the Mississippi River from La Crosse to St. Paul and was finally owned by the Davidson brothers of La Crosse. It appears that the boat was first commanded by William F. Davidson, but in 1862 the captain may have been James Newton. Information about the *Frank Steele* was supplied by Edwin Hill, curator, Murphy Library, University of Wisconsin at La Crosse, to present editor, 8 April 1980, and by James Hansen, reference librarian, State Historical Society of Wisconsin, to present editor, 23 May 1978.

3. The population of St. Paul in 1861 was about 10,700. According to John Sellar, who arrived at St. Paul on the same day as TM, "the Western town was flooded some 6 or 8 feet deep with water & every person had deserted the place. The East town is upon a bank some 80 to 90 feet above the level of the river" ("Journal," p. 6). A.L. Fortune noted that "St. Paul then boasted of the name of city with a few thousand of population and several substantial stone buildings. But most of the buildings were wood with paint on some. The site was pleasing on the banks of the river with a rolling land behind and plains to the west. St. Paul we thought should be a city but where could they have the cheap luxuries of the eastern cities and bear the cost of freighting so far inland was a question for the future to settle" ("Collection," p. 21).

4. The stage line operated by the J.C. and H.C. Burbank Company of St. Paul was "the customary means of transportation" to Georgetown. "It was an extremely tedious journey; we rode all day and when night came we pitched our tents, wrapped ourselves in our blankets & lay on the ground to sleep. The first night we camped out ice formed on a lake near by more than a quarter of an inch thick but I haven't suffered any from the cold" (Harkness to his wife Sabrina, 9 May 1862). Part of Cheadle's description

of the same journey undertaken two months later is both informative and amusing:

> From St. Paul a railway runs westward to St. Anthony, six miles distant—the commencement of the Great Pacific Railroad, projected to run across to California, and already laid out far on to the plains. From St. Anthony a "stage" wagon runs through the out-settlements of Minnesota as far as Georgetown. ... The "stage," a mere covered spring-wagon, was crowded and heavily laden. Inside were eight full-grown passengers and four children; outside six, in addition to the driver; on the roof an enormous quantity of luggage; and on the top of all were chained two huge dogs. ... The day was frightfully hot, and the passengers were packed so tightly, that it was only by the consent and assistance of his next neighbour that he [Cheadle] could free an arm to wipe the perspiration from his agonized countenance. Mosquitoes swarmed and feasted with impunity on the helpless crowd, irritating the four wretched babies into an incessant squalling, which the persevering singing of their German mothers about Fatherland was quite ineffectual to assuage. ... The dogs kept tumbling off their slippery perch (*North-West Passage by Land*, pp. 11-12).

A few days after this journey, in August 1862, the Minnesota Sioux uprising began and the stage to Georgetown was attacked, "the driver and passengers scalped, and the wagon thrown into Red River" (ibid., p. 160).

5. The little settlement of Georgetown is placed under cover of the belt of timber which clothes the banks of the river, while to the south and east endless prairie stretches away to the horizon. The place is merely a trading post of the Hudson's Bay Company, round which a few straggling settlers have established themselves. A company of Minnesota Volunteers was stationed here for the protection of the settlement against the Sioux. They were principally Irish or German Yankees; i.e., emigrants, outHeroding Herod in Yankeeism. ... These heroes, slovenly and unsoldier-like, yet full of swagger and braggadocio now, when the Sioux advanced to the attack on Fort Abercrombie, a few weeks afterwards, took refuge under beds, and hid in holes and corners, from whence they had to be dragged by their officers, who drew them out to face the enemy by putting revolvers to their heads (ibid., pp. 17-18).

    The captain of these unprepossessing soldiers, however, was kind enough to lend John Sellar's companions a large tent until they could make their own, a welcome gift because there was considerable rain during the long stay at Georgetown (see Sellar, "Journal," p. 17).

6. For more information about the *International* and her first load of passengers, see text note 11, below.

7. For a description of Dallas's visit and the ceremony organized by TM in honor of Dallas at Georgetown, see Introduction, p. xxiii, and notes 46 and 47 above.

8. But compare John Sellar's more jaundiced view of the Honourable Company's servants and practice:

    > A number of the company bought their saddles from the H.B. Company [at Edmonton] for which they were charged $3.50 while they actually were not worth more than 40C. Another act of the Keepers at Edmonton is worth notice, the first of the carts that came over they took advantage to buy for $10. & as soon as they heard that the carts were all for sale they put them down to $5—while they could not buy them out at the [Big Lake?] settlement for less than $20 such was the

Extortion they practiced all the way through the H.B. Territory ("Journal," pp. 71-72).

9. The Sioux lands west of the Mississippi had been ceded to the U.S. government, in return for regular payments of goods and food. For a number of years these payments had been incomplete, missing, or late. In August 1862, after waiting for six weeks, near starvation, at Fort Ridgeley, a band of Indians attacked the fort and the town of New Ulm. Sioux throughout Minnesota then rose against the white settlers. Many whites were killed, although J.J. Hargrave's estimate of 1,500 dead, which Wade quotes, is certainly greatly exaggerated. A modern estimate is 486 fatalities—360 civilians and 126 soldiers. For more information, see Hargrave, *Red River*, pp. 247-49; Wade, *Overlanders*, p. 170; Russell W. Fridley, *Minnesota: A History of the State* (St. Paul: University of Minnesota Press, 1975), p. 282; Milton and Cheadle, *North-West Passage by Land*, pp. 15-16, 160.

10. Milton and Cheadle describe the settlement as follows:

> Fort Garry . . . is situated on the north bank of the Assiniboine River, a few hundred yards above its junction with Red River. It consists of a square enclosure of high stone walls, flanked at each angle by round towers. Within this are several substantial wooden buildings— the Governor's residence, the gaol, and the storehouses for the Company's furs and goods. The shop, where articles of every description are sold, is thronged from morning till night by a crowd of settlers and half-breeds, who meet there to gossip and treat each other to rum and brandy, as well as to make their purchases.

> The Red River settlement extends beyond Fort Garry for about twenty miles to the northward along the banks of Red River, and about fifty to the westward along its tributary, the Assiniboine. The wealthier inhabitants live in large, well-built wooden houses, and the poorer half-breeds in rough log huts, or even Indian "lodges." There are several Protestant churches, a Romish cathedral and nunnery, and schools of various denominations. The neighbouring country is principally open, level prairie, the timber being confined, with a few exceptions, to the banks of the streams (*North-West Passage by Land*, pp. 35-36).

11. The *International* was not the first steamboat ever to visit Fort Garry. The *Anson Northup*, built by a Mississippi steamboatman of the same name at Lafayette (a point on the Red River opposite the mouth of the Cheyenne), arrived at the fort on 5 June 1859. The *Anson Northup* was renamed the *Pioneer* in 1861, but it sank at Cook's Creek below Fort Garry early in 1862.

The *International* was built for the J.C. and H.C. Burbank Company of St. Paul at a cost of about $20,000. Much of the materials and machinery for the new ship came from an older Mississippi River steamer, the *Freighter*. The *International* was 42 metres long and 8 metres wide, with a sternwheel 4.5 metres in diameter. The HBC controlled the operation of the steamer and in 1864 bought the *International* from the Burbanks. About 1873, when the U.S. Congress made it illegal for foreign-owned vessels to ply American rivers, the HBC transferred the boat to a company formed at St. Paul by its agent there, Norman Kittson. The HBC retained a controlling interest in this company until 1879. An unconfirmed secondary source states that the *International* was dismantled at Grand Forks, North Dakota, in 1880. The above information comes from Marion H. Herriot, "Steamboat Transportation on the Red River" (*Minnesota History* 21 [1940]: 245-71); Louis M. de Gryse, reference historian, Minnesota Historical Society at St. Paul, to present editor, 8 May 1980; Garron Wells, assistant archivist, HBCA, to present editor, 8 May 1980. More detailed history and references may be found in the Herriot article.

The arrival of the *International* with the Overlanders on board was reported by the *Fort Garry Nor'-Wester*, 28 May 1862, under the heading "Arrival of the Steamboat." The ship, noted the paper, drew only 38 centimetres when empty, but on this voyage, carrying 90 tonnes, drew 68 centimetres. One hundred and fifty passengers reached Fort Garry on the steamer, and "as they were gold-hunters and consequently had guns, they fired a right royal salute." Bishop Taché disembarked on the other side of the river, but the crowds were waiting on the side by the fort. "A complimentary address to the Captain was presented by the passengers, for his attention to them on the trip. The passengers were almost all gold-seekers, and a more respectable body of men could not be found anywhere." The newspaper carried the names of the passengers, and almost all were indeed Overlanders.

12. James McKay (?-1879) was the son of an HBC officer, James McKay, and was born at Edmonton House of a native or Métis mother. In the service of the HBC, the younger McKay established Qu'Appelle Lakes Post in 1854 and was later moved to Fort Pelly. In 1859 he went to St. Paul to guide Governor Simpson on his first journey by the Red River route to Rupert's Land. Simpson tried to persuade McKay to remain in the company service, but McKay appears to have left the HBC about 1860 to become an "important plains trader" (Rich, *Hudson's Bay Company*, 2:896). Lord Southesk described McKay in detail, and he was an admired friend, interpreter, and guide to Palliser in 1857. This "very large and intelligent half-breed" was familiarly known as "Big Jim" (Spry, *Palliser Papers*, p. lxvi). He later served on the Council of Assiniboia and on the North West Council. Between 1871 and 1878 he was a member of Manitoba's legislative council, president of the executive council, speaker, and minister of agriculture. For an anecdotal (and unflattering) account of the part played by the "Honourable James" in the negotiations before the signing

of Treaty No. Six with the prairie Indians, see Erasmus, *Buffalo Days and Nights*, pp. 240-43 (see also Spry, *Palliser Papers*, pp. lxvi-lxvii, 601; Southesk, *Saskatchewan and the Rocky Mountains*, pp. 8, 9, 12; Allan R. Turner, "James McKay," *DCB* 10:473-74).

13. Jane Dallas (1839-1909), née Douglas, second daughter of Amelia Connolly and Sir James Douglas, was born at Fort Vancouver and married Alexander Grant Dallas (see introduction note 31) in 1858. They had nine children, one of whom died in infancy. On board the *International*, Richard Alexander described the "pleasure of talking a good while the other day" to Mrs. Dallas. It "seemed to be a link to civilization to *see* a lady here, much more to talk to one is a perfect Godsend" (*Diary and Narrative*, p. 6). Lady Dallas was accompanied on the steamboat by her maid and piper. She was the mother of one child (Mary Jane, born in 1861) at the time. One day, she was "heard lamenting to Bishop Taché the slow progress that was being made, and also how tired she was of the hard fare, consisting chiefly of pork and beans, which was about the extent of the larder on board the *International*" (McNaughton, *Overland to Cariboo*, p. 23). Taché's presence on board the *International* is not mentioned by TM, but Alexander Fortune noted that the "Bishop had been in Europe and was on his way back with several young priests and brothers destined for mission work in the Great Lone Land" ("Collection," p. 24. See also introduction note 45).

14. William Mactavish (1815-70) was born in Edinburgh and emigrated to Rupert's Land in 1833 as an apprentice with the HBC. He served first at Norway House and was soon on his way up the company's ladder of command in North America. He had excellent connections in the fur trade, being a nephew to Chief Factor John George McTavish, whose father was a friend of Simon McTavish of the North West Company. William's sister Letitia married James Hargrave, under whom

William served at York Factory. William was placed in charge of Sault Ste. Marie, and later York Factory, where in 1852 he became chief factor. In 1856 Mactavish became officer in charge of Upper Fort Garry. He married there and in 1858 was appointed governor of Assiniboia, though he once said he would rather have been "a stoker in Hell." His reluctance was justified, for he considered himself a good fur-trade administrator but a poor politician, and yet he had charge of the settlement at what was politically the most difficult time in its history. At George Simpson's death in 1860 Mactavish was appointed acting governor of Rupert's Land. He was relieved of this position in 1862 with the arrival of the new governor, Alexander Dallas, but when Dallas resigned in 1864 Mactavish again took up the post. During the events leading up to the rebellion of 1869, Mactavish's performance attracted criticism from all sides, though he tried to be fair and to act in what he considered the best interests of the settlers and Métis inhabitants as well as of the company. Weak and ailing, he was imprisoned for a short while by Riel, and at that time he resigned from the HBC. On his release in February, 1870, he sailed for home but died just after landing in England. For more information see N. Jaye Goossen, "William Mactavish," *DCB* 9:529; Rich, *Hudson's Bay Company*, 2:896; Spry, *Palliser Papers*, p. 602.

William J. Christie (1824-ca. 1886), member of a well-known fur-trade family and country-born son of Chief Factor Alexander Christie, who was once governor of Assiniboia, entered the HBC in 1843. In 1854 he became chief factor in the Swan River district and in 1858 chief factor in charge of the Saskatchewan district. In 1868 William was promoted to the rank of inspecting chief factor and, later, to supervisor. Before retiring in 1870 to Brockville, Ontario, he served as a commissioner in the treaty negotiations with the Saskatchewan district Indians.

Christie was in charge of Edmon-

ton House when the Palliser party was there in 1858-59 and helped Palliser in organizing his "goods for payment, and paid the men, a most troublesome office" (Spry, *Palliser Papers*, p. 594). In fact, Christie was a rather colourful character. Once, when he was in charge of Edmonton and the fort was surrounded by angry Blackfeet determined to avenge an attack on their camp by Crees, he tried to don his ceremonial sword for the first time in many years, the better to impress his audience during bargaining talks. But he found it no longer fit, and his corpulent middle had to be forcibly strapped in by his laughing helpers. Christie also sent for Father Lacombe, who spent the night walking around the exterior of the fort reasoning at the top of his voice in the Blackfoot tongue with the hidden Indians (see Katherine Hughes, *Father Lacombe: The Blackrobe Voyageur* [New York: Moffat, Yard & Co., 1911], p. 178). In March, 1859, Christie and Dr. Hector of the Palliser expedition set off from Edmonton to Fort Pitt to bring medical help to the agent there, Louis Chastellain (whom the Overlanders met later in 1862). Although travelling with two of the best guides on the plains—one was Peter Erasmus—Christie and Hector got lost, ran out of food, and began going in circles. They were saved when they stumbled on some native people. For more on Christie, see "The Christie Family and the HBC," *Beaver*, 3, no. 11 (1923): 417-19; "The Men of Hudson's Bay: Oldtime Fur Trade Officers of the 'Great Company', VII," ibid., p. 402; Erasmus, *Buffalo Days and Nights*, pp. 96-97.

For more information on Taché, see introduction note 45; on Love, introduction note 26; and on Whitford, introduction note 26 also.

15. For more information about Rochette, see introduction note 44.

16. Griffith Owen Corbett was ordained 19 December 1852, "the second man sent out by the Colonial and Continental Church Society," and "was placed in charge of Holy Trinity, Headlingley, then a new church to the west of the present city

of Winnipeg" (T.C.B. Boon, *The Anglican Church from the Bay to the Rockies* [Toronto: Ryerson, 1962], p. 83). Corbett served at Fort Garry from 1853-55 and from 1857-62. Late in 1862 he was charged in a scandalous court case involving a maid-servant in his home. He was convicted and sentenced to six months' imprisonment, but his friends, who thought he had been framed for his agitation against the HBC government and in favour of the establishment of a crown colony at Red River, organized a jailbreak. (Corbett had some years earlier testified before the British House of Commons committee investigating the HBC that the company had neglected the church at the settlement. He had by his own admission demonstrated an "unceasing hostility" to the company. A petition for his release circulated in 1862 was signed by 420 Red River inhabitants, but it was denied.) After the jailbreak, interestingly enough, Corbett continued to live unmolested at Red River for a full year before returning to England, where he was minister at Egloskerry, Cornwall, 1868-69, and at St. Mary's Church, Cambridgeshire, 1875-76. For more details see Morton, *Canadian West*, pp. 819, 859-60; Hargrave, *Red River*, pp. 260-74, 280-89; *Crockford's Clerical Directory for 1890* (London: Horace Cox, 1890), p. 284.

John Black (1818-82) was born at Dumfries, Scotland, and educated at Knox College, Toronto. He was ordained in 1851 and immediately sent to Red River, where he began to minister to the Scots at Kildonan. This was a victory for the Presbyterians at the settlement, for they had long resented the fact that the HBC refused to help them obtain their own minister. Black later acted as a moderating force in the rebellion of 1869-70. He died at Kildonan in Manitoba. Margaret McNaughton provides the following additional information about Black's sermon to the Overlanders: "The sermon by Mr. Black was one to be remembered, and produced a deep impression upon the minds of all who heard it. The text was from Revelation iii.18: 'I

counsel thee to buy of me gold tried in the fire, that thou mayest be rich' " (*Overland to Cariboo*, p. 28). For more information on Black, see Rich, *Hudson's Bay Company*, 2:558-59, 926; Wallace, *Macmillan DCB*, p. 59; Morton, *Canadian West*, pp. 804, 904. For the history of the Selkirk settlers' thirty-year struggle for a Scottish minister, see Alexander Ross, *The Red River Settlement: Its Rise, Progress, and Present State* (London: Smith, Elder and Co., 1856); Hargrave, *Red River*.

17. The *Fort Garry Nor'Wester* of 11 June 1862 reported that "a Norwegian" in the service of the HBC had drowned in the river opposite Fort Garry on "the Sunday before last." The body was found the following day. "We will not say that this was a summary judgement for profaning that day, but it might be so, and is certainly a warning."

18. For more information about the Red River cart and its use on the prairie and a discussion of the route taken by TM's company of Overlanders, see "A Note on the Trail," Appendix 2.

19. In 1857 White Horse Plain appeared to the experienced eye of H.Y. Hind as

a vast, slightly undulating prairie, bounded by the horizon in every direction but the south, where the distant wooded banks of the Assiniboine afford some relief to the eye. The grass is long and rank, and the soil a black mould of great depth, often exceeding eighteen inches. In many places it is thrown up into conical heaps by moles, and uniformly displays the same rich appearance, truly represented by the bountiful profusion of verdure it sustains (*Exploring Expeditions* (1:147).

White Horse Plain had been a centre of Métis population since about 1814. The Métis leader Cuthbert Grant had been given a tract of land there by the HBC, and about 1820 he was made a "Warden of the Plains" to help secure his loyalty and that of his followers who had taken part in the massacre at Seven Oaks.

Grant was a leader of the annual buffalo hunt, and Métis from Red River gathered at White Horse Plain at the start of that event, but the great rendezvous for the hunt was at Pembina.

After the Sioux uprising was put down in the U.S. late in 1862 (see note 9 above), numbers of the Indians moved to Red River and settled at White Horse Plain, alarming the other settlers.

Today Grantown, the centre of the settlement, is known as St. François-Xavier. For more details, see Rich, *Hudson's Bay Company*, 2:515, 857; Morton, *Canadian West*, pp. 641, 645, 658-59; Spry, *Palliser Papers*, p. 166n.

The trading post mentioned by TM was White Horse Plain or Lane's Post at Pigeon Lake. It was built in the 1850's and first appears in HBC records in 1856, when clerk William D. Lane was in charge.

According to Joseph James Hargrave it was established "chiefly with a view to farming operations" and was located "about five miles beyond the church [St. François-Xavier]."

William Lane remained in charge of this post until at least 1871. We have been unable to trace the name of the servant in charge of this post between 1871 and 1874. Mr. Lane was appointed Chief Trader in 1864.

During the next nine years the following men were appointed in charge of this post: William Clark, Clerk, 1874-1875; E.W. Gigot, Clerk, 1875-1877; and Henry Moncrieff, Salesman, 1877-1883 (Garron Wells, assistant archivist, HBCA, to present editor, 8 May 1980).

H.Y. Hind was "very hospitably entertained" by William Lane at this post in September 1857 (*Exploring Expeditions*, 1:148).

20. The degree of the Overlanders' thirst may also be gauged by the fact that the water of Long Lake "was so impure as to be almost unfit for use. Before using it was strained through cloths, which process but partially made the liquid drinkable" (McNaughton, *Overland to Cariboo*, p. 34).

21. As mentioned above (introduction note 26) evidence from the HBC's Fort Edmonton Journal indicates that there were twenty men in Symington's group and sixty-three in the Redgrave-Love-Flett party. There were actually three companies of Overlanders besides TM's (see Introduction, p. xxi).

22. More is known about some members of the committee than about others. Joseph Halpenny was accompanied on the 1862 trip by his two brothers, William and John. In December, 1863, Dobson Prest wrote home from Victoria that Joseph was "working at the Carpenter trade with me." Nothing more was heard of Joseph in British Columbia, but his brother William Halpenny (ca. 1830-96) remained in the province for the rest of his life. In William's obituary in the *Colonist*, 8 November 1896, the writer noted that "poor old William Halpenny" had been one of the Overlanders of '62, and "though he made money, did not keep it" and died destitute. "He was known in his former years as one of the best guides in the province" and had often been employed on government exploring and mapping expeditions.

Wattie was James Wattie (1829-1907), who also travelled with a brother, William (1842-1918). James was born in Scotland and had already spent three years in California from 1852 to 1855. William had been an apprentice machinist in Montreal. When they arrived in British Columbia, James accompanied A.L. Fortune to Williams Creek in the fall of 1862. A few weeks later, Fortune and the Wattie brothers travelled from Alexandria to Bella Coola through the Chilcotin. They were the only Overlanders to reach the Pacific Coast by this dangerous route (see introduction note 17). The next year the Watties went back to Cariboo where they did well; they obtained a claim on Williams Creek and were associated with "Cariboo" Cameron. When James, who was foreman on Cameron's claim, left to return east in 1864, his friends gave him a lavish farewell dinner and subscribed $374 for a parting gift of a gold watch. William, who remained one year longer, was managing director of the Bed Rock Drain Co. and active in the affairs of the Williams Creek Hospital and of the Reading Room. The Watties were equally successful back in the east. James became operator of a woollen mill at Valleyfield, Quebec, and William became a machinist and later superintendent of mills in Massachusetts, where "he invented and patented over sixty devices relating to weaving machinery" (see Wade, *Overlanders*, pp. 161-62; news items in the *Colonist*, 26 December 1864, 6 January 1865, 18 November 1866; Vertical File, PABC).

For Wallace, see introduction note 29. Morrow was William W. Morrow, whose ox "Buck" ran his owner over at the Qu'Appelle River crossing and later kicked him in the face while Morrow was trying to pack the unruly beast at Lac Ste Anne, compelling the unlucky victim to remain behind there until Dr. Symington's party arrived. In British Columbia Morrow went into partnership with A.L. Fortune, setting up the Overland Restaurant at Victoria (see introduction note 17 on Fortune): "Board $5 per week, $1 per day, dinner 3 bits, supper 2 bits," as advertised in the *Colonist* (5 March 1863 to 31 March 1864). Morrow later went mining in the Kootenay district and was on Wild Horse Creek in 1874 and Perry Creek in 1878 (see Fortune, "Collection," p. 8; Schubert, "Reminiscences," p. 15).

Phillips was Thomas Phillips (ca. 1836-?), son of a physician, Dr. George H. Phillips, of Ormstown near Montreal. He was accompanied by his brother, William (1840-1919), who left a short autobiography and "Reminiscences 1840-1916" (typescript copy, PABC) covering the events of 1862. Both Phillips brothers left B.C. immediately after their arrival in 1862, proceeding to California where William mined for a time. Thomas settled in Morris, Illinois. William tried his hand at a variety of occupations, settled as a

lumber business manager in Texas, and eventually retired to San Diego. Fortune was Alexander, not William Fortune (see introduction note 17).

Simpson may have been the D. Simpson who, according to Begg (*History of British Columbia*, p. 447), was still living in B.C. in 1889. But nothing more is known of him, unless we can assume that he was identical to the D.F. Simpson arrested by Constable Redgrave (probably the Overlander) for attacking a ticket-taker at a Victoria theatre in January, 1863 (see *Colonist*, 3, 7, and 9 January 1863).

Little is known of Joseph Hough, but in his December, 1863, letter to his brother, Prest commented: "Joseph Huff has been sick on William Creek for a long time,' sometimes better, sometimes worse, the last I heard poor Joe's means had run out, and he was forced to go to hospital somewhat better than he had been."

Adolphus Urlin (1816-?), an Englishman who had emigrated to Southwold about 1840, and his son Alfred John Urlin (1840-?), crossed the plains together in 1862; but the father returned to Wallacetown, C.W., in 1864, and the son settled in Missoula, Montana (Wade, *Overlanders*, p. 169).

Arthur C. Robertson was a civil engineer, son of the jail-keeper at Goderich, C.W. (see ibid; Dobson Prest to father from Victoria, December 1862).

23. "Soft River" has not been positively identified. John Hunniford called it "Fly Creek" in his journal. It may have been a name given by the guide to what is now known as Squirrel Creek, which lies about this point on the old trail.

24. Points Creek is possibly identical with today's Pine Creek, which was described by R.H. Alexander of the Redgrave party under date of 19 June: "We crossed Pine Creek easily as the bottom was good and hard" (*Diary and Narrative*, p. 9). The Carlton Trail did cross Pine Creek at approximately the distance mentioned from Fort Garry.

25. The beautiful creek which took so long to cross was probably the

Whitemud River, which intersects the old trail in this vicinity.

26. The Minnedosa River appears on one of H.Y. Hind's 1858 maps as the Little Saskatchewan or Rapid River ("A Map to Illustrate a Narrative of the Canadian Red River Exploring Expedition of 1857, and of the Assiniboine and Saskatchewan Exploring Expeditions of 1858. By Henry Youle Hind, M.S., F.R.G.S." Facing p. 9 of Hind, *Exploring Expeditions*, Vol. 1).

27. The lake at which the Overlanders stopped is probably identical with the one called, appropriately, Salt Lake, which lies near the old trail about 16 kilometres east of Shoal Lake. The salt springs mentioned by the guide may have been those worked by James Monkman's sons at Lake Winnipegosis or the deposits worked for the HBC at Swan River. Both of these operations were located a considerable distance north of Salt Lake, but they were the largest salt works supplying the Red River settlement at the time. The native people collected salt at Turtle River on Dauphin Lake and at Crane River on Lake Manitoba. Both of these places were closer to the Overlanders' trail than the commercial salt works mentioned. There were salt deposits at other places close to the settlement, for example, near Stony Mountain, but these were not worked in early years. For more information, see Hind, *Exploring Expeditions*, 1:279; 2:43-46, 291-94. The Hind map cited in note 26 above shows Monkman's salt works near the southern end, eastern arm, of Lake Winnipegosis.

28. Arrow River is called Clearwater Creek by John Sellar ("Journal," p. 32). Birdtail River is called Wind or Wing River by R.B. McMicking ("Journal," p. 9); it is now known as Birdtail Creek. Sellar calls it Rappid River in his diary (p. 38).

29. *Assiniboin* is an Ojibwa word meaning "one who cooks by means of stones" (*A Dictionary of Canadianisms on Historical Principals* [Toronto: Gage, 1967]).

30. John Palliser wrote of the Assiniboine River crossing here, which he made in August 1857:

The valley of the Assineboine is depressed to 250 feet below the prairie level, and is about three-quarters of a mile in breadth. On the eastern side of the river it is marshy with swamp, but on the western side, which is slightly elevated above it at this place, it is dry and produces fine grass for the feeding of cattle. The river banks are composed of sand of a light brown colour, and at this point the river averages 15 feet in depth and 60 yards across. . . . The prairie level on either bank is reached by ascending the very steep slopes which are covered with dense wood, and which enclose the river between them: it is a great task for loaded carts to effect this ascent (Spry, *Palliser Papers*, p. 123).

31. The "dilapidated" old Fort Ellice which the Overlanders visited had been established in 1831 overlooking Beaver Creek; the new fort was being built on a plateau above the junction of the Qu'Appelle and Assiniboine Rivers. Palliser wrote in 1857 that the fort once "was a very lucrative emporium of the fur trade, but now its principal value is derived from its importance as a post for trading provisions . . . the whole of the trade in the country, both that of the Hudson Bay Company and also of those engaged in opposition, pass by the fort, so that the . . . Company often obtain indirectly considerable advantage from their rivals . . . who are frequently obliged to exchange the furs traded by them from the Indians for the common necessaries of life, which can only be obtained at this fort" (ibid., pp. 122-23).

32. Little is known about William McKay, the master of Fort Ellice in 1862. Milton and Cheadle were "very kindly entertained" by him in September of 1862 when they passed this way (*North-West Passage by Land*, p. 52).

33. The *Oxford Dictionary* defines a *bawbee* as a "Scotch coin of base silver equivalent originally to three and afterwards to six pennies of Scotch money, or a half-penny

English." McMicking presumably means McKay was careful with money.

34. James Settee (ca. 1817-1902) was one of four native Indian boys taken for training by Reverend John West at the Anglican Church Missionary School at Red River, when Settee was about six years old. Settee himself was of Swampy Cree origin. In 1841 he was teaching school at Park's Creek, and in 1842 he was sent to Beaver Creek near Fort Ellice. A year or two after the mission at Beaver Creek closed, Settee was sent to help the Reverend James Hunter at The Pas and at Lac la Ronge. In 1853, partly because of his great success in attracting native converts, he was ordained at Red River. In 1861 the district of Swan River was placed under Reverend William Stagg, assisted by Settee, who worked throughout the country around Fort Pelly and the Touchwood Hills until 1867. After that Settee seems to have become an itinerant missionary, working at many different posts— Split Lake in the Nelson River district, Lac la Ronge again, Prince Albert, Nepowewin, The Pas, and at Jackhead on the west side of Lake Winnipeg. He retired to East St. Peter's but continued to do some work in the region south of the lake. He died in Winnipeg.

Settee was the second native Indian to be ordained in the Church of England (the first was Henry Budd). He was said to be of medium height, thickset, vigorous, and of a happy disposition. He and his wife Sarah Cook, whom he married in 1835, had a large family.

H.Y. Hind met Settee at the Qu'Appelle Mission in 1858 and described a service there: "The Rev. Mr. Settee read the prayers in English with great ease and correctness; he preached in Ojibway, and a hymn was sung in the Cree language." Hind had much to say about the difficulties of Settee's position as a Swampy Cree hoping to convert Plains Cree people to Christianity (*Exploring Expeditions*, 1:321-25). For more information, see T.C.B. Boon, "James Settee—Travelling

Missionary of the Plains," *These Men Went Out* (Toronto: Ryerson, n.d.), pp. 59-60; William Bertal Heeney, ed., "James Settee," *Leaders of the Canadian Church*, Second Series (Toronto: Musson, 1920), pp. 73-78.

35. Dobson Prest, who was helping Morrow hold his cart back, reported to his father in a letter written at Edmonton, 22 July 1862, that Morrow was "thrown crosswise of the track the cart wheel passing over his head cutting his ear in three pieces."

36. Until now very little had come to light about Dr. Edward Stevenson. His presence must have comforted the travellers, and he attended Eustace Pattison before Pattison's death of diphtheria at Fort George. James Schubert states that Stevenson "settled in practise" at New Westminster ("Reminiscences," p. 10). The following advertisement appears in the *British Columbian* of 1 November 1862, but disappears after 10 December of that year: "E. Stevenson, M.D., Licentiate Canada, Having arrived *via* Overland Route, begs to acquaint the inhabitants of New Westminster that he has established himself for practice in their City. Office, in the building lately occupied by Barnard's Express." The editor of the newspaper commented in the same issue that "Dr. Stevenson, whose card will be found elsewhere, arrived recently with the party which came overland from Canada, and has decided to settle amongst us. We have examined his credentials, and find that having passed an examination before the Medical Board of Upper Canada, he holds a license to practise Medicine, Surgery, and Midwifery, signed by Sir Edmund Head, late Governor General of Canada and the Maritime Provinces. Dr. Stevenson has had three years successful practice in the town of Belville, C.W., and, we learn from other sources, stood well in his profession there."

A letter to the editor of the *British Columbian* from Stevenson, which was published on 25 October 1862 and seems to be the first reference to the Overlander journey to appear in its pages is reproduced here. It is also interesting because Stevenson's conclusions regarding the suitability of the overland route are quite different from McMicking's in the present narrative:

THE OVERLAND ROUTE

Mr. Editor,—Having heard much during my short residence in this Country of *trails* and *roads*, and much which has been interesting and instructive, I purpose, sir, with your permission, to give you, in a brief manner, some ideas respecting a trail which I with others have travelled during the present season, in the hope, by so doing, of adding to the general stock of information respecting these means of communication to and in this new Country—I allude to the trail from Canada, through the Hudson Bay Territory, to British Columbia. The bare mention of this trail, sir, will be quite sufficient to convince you without any farther evidence on my part, that, in point of *length* it carries off the palm from anything of the kind in this Country. I have travelled the longest of them; and it merely seemed to me as though, after having read a very large book, I found it necessary to read a short appendix in order to reach the end.

With our face towards the setting sun, attracted by the reputed richness of the gold fields of Cariboo, for five long months did we wend our way, by rail and by steamboat, by stage and by ox-cart, by packtrain and on foot, by canoe and by raft, and last of all by personal packing. As it is foreign to my intention to give a detailed account of the trip, I will merely state to you that, to my mind, there are just two objections to the route in question being, *in its present condition*, travelled by emigrants, viz: The great length of

time, and the unnecessary hardships therein involved. Why spend five months in reaching this Country when it can be reached in about half the time and about the same expense by another route? Why wade to the knees in mud, day after day, for weeks together, and to the waist—nay, *swim*—once or twice and sometimes oftener, every day, for several hundred miles of the journey, when one may come the whole way without wetting his foot? Others may make the journey in four and a half, *possibly* in four months, but I defy them to do it in less. They cannot start from Red River before June 1st, the grass not being sufficiently long for the cattle before that time; so that the mining season will be nearly or quite over before they can reach the end of their journey. Might they not as well be here in proper season? I do not wish, sir, to exaggerate the difficulties of this route; but I think it is only right that things should be spoken of as they are found, and in writing this I am but giving expression to the sentiments of every one of the overland party.

Respectfully yours,
E. Stevenson, M.D.
New Westminster, B.C.
Oct. 22, 1862

37. Gulch Creek may be identical with today's Cutarm Creek, which was shown as Big Cut-arm Creek on Palliser's map and Great Cutarm Creek on H.Y. Hind's map. In his diary entry for 28 June 1862, Richard Alexander, travelling with the Redgrave party, describes the crossing of "Big Cut Arm Creek" close to the same point on the trail and notes the steep hills on both sides. In his entry for 29 June, Alexander mentions that "yesterday Love prospected on Cut Arm Creek and found gold" (*Diary and Narrative,* p. 10). The steep sides of the stream may account for TM's appellation "Gulch Creek," but that name cannot be found in old

gazetteers. H.Y. Hind's companion, J.A. Dickinson, described the "Big Cut Arm" as flowing "in a valley 1200 feet broad and 180 feet deep, resembling that of the Qu'Appelle" ("Mr. Dickinson's Narrative," *Exploring Expeditions*, 1:423).

38. The deserted post of Touchwood Hills was situated "about six miles north and two miles west of the present town of Punnichy. In 1861 a new post had been built about fourteen miles south, near an Indian Mission on the western side of the Little Touchwood Hills" (Russell, *Carlton Trail*, p. 35). "The country around Fort Ellice and the Touchwood Hills is well adapted for cultivation, and the rearing of cattle; the soil is good, but there is a great scarcity of timber either for fuel or building purposes" (Captain John Palliser, quoted in Spry, *Palliser Papers*, p. 527). The Touchwood Hills "or Montagnes de Tondre, consist of easy undulating hills, in height under 400 feet, well wooded, however, and containing lakes varying in size from about three-quarters to an acre and a quarter in surface" (ibid., p. 163).

The "immense, trackless prairie" which TM mentions a few lines later was probably the region aptly called the "Carry Wood Plain" (see Hind, *Exploring Expeditions*, 1:411). For an excellent general description of the Touchwood Hills region, see ibid., pp. 412-20.

39. The high hills TM mentions are possibly the Minichinas Hills, west of present day Wakaw, Saskatchewan, or other hills in the near vicinity (see "A Note on the Trail").

40. "A General Map of the Routes in British North America Explored by the Expedition under Captain Palliser during the Years 1857, 1858, 1859, 1860. Compiled from the Observations and Reports of Captain Palliser and his Officers, including the Maps constructed by Dr. Hector, and other authentic documents. To accompany The Journals, Detailed Reports, and Observations' Presented to both Houses of Parliament, by Command of Her Majesty, 19 May 1863" indicates that at this crossing

place the South Saskatchewan River was "230 yards wide, swift and deep, with a beach." The crossing place was near present-day Batoche (see Russell, *Carlton Trail*, p. 8).

41. Kelso's Christian name was apparently James, not Robert (according to A.L. Fortune and M.S. Wade, although Wade calls him Robert in one place). A few details of Kelso's early years in B.C. have survived. In "Overland Trek Recalls Another," by R.W. Harrison (*Vancouver Sun*, 30 September 1947), the author states that about 1907 he met and stayed with John Malcolm (?-1910), another Acton Overlander, in a cabin at Keithley Creek. Malcolm told Harrison that he had been born in Scotland and emigrated to New York as a young man, where he worked as a bookkeeper. Becoming ill, he was advised to seek the northern woods, so he moved to Canada and shortly after joined the Overlanders. Malcolm stated that he and James Kelso were among those of the party who stayed at Edmonton in the fall of 1862, where Malcolm worked for the HBC at the winter horse camp at Battle River. In the spring he and Kelso and Sam Kyse prospected a bit around Jasper, then drifted on to Cariboo, and in fact these men were probably the party of three who immediately preceded Milton and Cheadle on their journey through the mountains in the summer of 1863 (see *North-West Passage by Land*, pp. 222, 238-39, 262). Kelso mined at Grouse and Harvey Creeks in the Cariboo for a time; Malcolm does not mention his ultimate fate. Sam Kyse sold his apparently unprofitable claim on Keithley Creek to a Chinese miner who made $33,000 from it. Malcolm became a clerk at Lillooet in 1864 and in 1866 accompanied A.L. Fortune (Harrison says William Fortune, but this is incorrect) to the Big Bend mines. He then took up land at Spallumcheen but apparently did not farm there. He was back at Harvey Creek in 1868 and remained there until his death at Barkerville.

William Strachan, from London, C.W., and George Reid, a blacksmith from Huntingdon, C.E., were assisted in Kelso's rescue by one of the Phillips brothers. According to John Sellar: "Thomas Phillips" with Strachan and Reid "made a rush for the scene of distress" and "just got forward in time to save [Kelso] from a watery grave" ("Journal," p. 52). But William Phillips asserted in his memoirs that it was he and not his brother who assisted in this emergency ("Reminiscences 1840-1916," p. 22). Strachan, ironically, was the one Overlander later drowned in the North Thompson River.

42. According to popular first-aid texts of the time, the "usual remedies" consisted of first removing the victim to shelter, stripping, drying and warming the body, and clearing the mouth and throat. Artificial respiration might then be begun if a doctor was present, using a bellows-like instrument inserted in one nostril while the other nostril was held closed and the windpipe "gently depressed" to prevent air from entering the stomach. In the absence of a physician, according to Newton Bosworth, laymen might "endeavour to assist the natural breathing . . . by pressure on the thorax, ribs, and abdominal muscles . . . merely by the hands, so as to press out as large a portion of the internal air as possible; and then *removing* and *applying* the pressure alternately." Stimulants such as "heartshorn, vinegar, mustard and warm negus" were also used, and sometimes bleeding was resorted to as well (see Newton Bosworth, *The Accidents of Human Life* [London: Thomas Ward and Co., 1834], pp. 88-96; Sir Arthur Clarke, *A Code of Instructions for the Treatment of Sufferers from Railroad and Steamboat Accidents* [Dublin: Alexander Thom, 1849], pp. 9-16).

43. Carlton House was situated in a position to take advantage of the nearby buffalo hunting-grounds of the south and also of the fur-producing areas to the north. From this post pemmican was sent for the northern fur brigades. However, according to Milton and Cheadle, "as the fur-bearing animals have decreased in the woods, and the buffalo are often far distant on the plains, it has ceased to be one of the most profitable establishments." According to the same writers, Carlton consisted of a "few wooden buildings, surrounded by a high square palisade, flanked at each corner with small square towers," and stood on "the low ground close to the river, and below the high banks which formed the ancient boundary of the stream" *(North-West Passage by Land,* p. 58). It was originally established by William Tomison at the end of the eighteenth century, and the last fort at Carlton was destroyed by fire during the rebellion of 1885. For more information on Carlton House, see Rich, *Hudson's Bay Company,* 2:369; Morton, *Canadian West,* p. 697; Russell, *Carlton Trail,* p. 8.

The agent in charge of Carlton House in 1862, whom McMicking does not mention by name, was Alexander Lillie. Lillie had been in charge of Lower Fort Garry when Palliser arrived there in July 1857. Later he was promoted to the position of chief trader, and "saw long service with the Hudson's Bay Company in the Lower Red River district, Cumberland House and Lac la Pluie" (Spry, *Palliser Papers,* p. 600).

44. The Thickwood Hills are an extensive range lying in the area north of present-day North Battleford and extending in a northwesterly direction to the vicinity of St. Walburg. The Lumpy Hills have not been identified. Since it would not have been possible for the Overlanders to pass the Thickwood Hills in a single day, what TM calls the Lumpy Hills may have formed part of the same range. This supposition is supported by maps and information supplied by D'Arcy Hande, of Saskatoon, and Edwin C. Morgan, of Regina, both of the Saskatchewan Archives Board. Dr. Ian Dyck, supervisor of archeological research for the Saskatchewan Department of Culture and Youth, has pointed out that a "Lumpy Hill of the Woods" is designated on the Carlton Trail just east of the South Branch crossing on H.Y. Hind's 1858

map (also on Palliser's map of the region), and suggests that in writing about hills in the general area some months after passing there, TM simply confused their names (Dr. Ian Dyck to present editor, 24 October 1979). A.L. Fortune described the Thickwood Hills as "high plateaus like a mountainous region with some timber on them" ("Collection," p. 35).

45. It was common experience for travellers in this part of the country to be followed by wolves, but whether these which followed the Over-landers were the large timber or "thick-wood wolves," the grey wolves or "buffalo-runners," or the prairie wolves or "coyotes," cannot be determined from TM's narrative. According to E.T. Seton, the grey wolves almost disappeared when the buffalo vanished in the 1870's and 1880's, but they began to increase again when settlers brought cattle to the plains (*Life Histories of Northern Animals: An Account of the Mammals of Manitoba* [New York: Scribner's, 1909], 2:752, 754). In early days, the grey wolves formed constant escorts to the great Métis wagon trains on the annual buffalo hunt and to other cart trains carrying meat and pemmican. The terrain between Carlton and Fort Pitt would seem better suited to timber-wolves, however. Milton and Cheadle describe a buffalo hunt in this region late in 1862, where "it was curious to see how the wolves seemed to spring up, as it were, out of the ground, at the sound of the first shot. Two or three appeared on every little eminence, where they sat watching the progress of the hunt" (*North-West Passage by Land*, p. 63; see also Spry, *Palliser Papers*, pp. 112, 145, 176).

46. Fort Pitt, which stood about thirty miles northeast of the present town of Lloydminster, Saskatchewan, was first used in 1835. The area in which it lay was rich in buffalo even when there was a shortage at Carlton and Edmonton. Gardens produced well there, though farming was not carried on with vigour around the post in 1862. A small amount of fur-trading was also done. Dr. James

Hector described the fort, which was smaller than Carlton, as it looked in 1857: "Fort Pitt stands on the left bank of the river, which runs past it to the north. . . . The total absence of wood within sight of the fort strikes one very much, but there is abundance of timber to be had a short distance to the N.W. The fort is built upon a flat about 20 feet above the river level, which is of very considerable extent, and merges by a gentle slope into the high lands behind. . . . This feature, along with the hilly aspect of the country across the river, gives the situation a very open and pleasant look" (Spry, *Palliser Papers*, p. 195). See also Milton and Cheadle, *North-West Passage by Land*, pp. 169-70.

47. The agent in charge at Fort Pitt was Louis Chastellain, a Métis fur-trade veteran. His marriage on 21 August 1838 was blessed by Father François Norbert Blanchet, who was on his famous tour through the Northwest with Father Modeste Demers. It was recorded thus: "Louis Chastelain, engagé, domiciled at Fort Carleton, of-age son of Jacques Chatelain and of ———, Cree, on the one part, and Geneviève Savoyard . . . of-age daughter of Pierre Savoyard and Marguerite Sauteuse." The bride "has not known how to sign"; the groom "has signed with us" (*Catholic Church Records of the Pacific Northwest* [St. Paul, Oregon: French Prairie Press, 1972], pp. 2-3). Chastellain was mentioned by Dr. Hector of the Palliser expedition and also by Milton and Cheadle, and his hospitality and friendliness were noted. It may have been these qualities which had prompted Dr. Hector, in company with William Christie, to make such a determined effort to reach Chastellain from Edmonton when he fell ill at Fort Pitt in March 1859 (see text note 14 above).

McMicking does not mention it, but the Overlanders had already lost the trail once, on 4 July, a day before reaching what they "supposed to be Pike [presumably now Jackfish] Lake" on the way between Carlton and Pitt. R.B. McMicking noted that this caused some delay as they

searched for the path ("Journal," p.
15). John Sellar describes a general
meeting of the company at Fort Pitt
on 9 July, "to make some new
travelling laws as we were just about
to enter the country where the
Blackfeet & Cree Indians were fight-
ing & where they had striped a party
of whites but a few days previous, &
sent them back nacked" ("Journal,"
p. 59). Some of the resolutions
adopted stipulated that guns be kept
at the ready, that the company travel
in closer order, and that a guide be
engaged.

Hugh Dempsey has identified
"Mitchelle" as Michel Callihoo,
born "about 1825, the son of an
Iroquois who had been brought west
from the Caughnawauga Band near
Montreal as a hunter and trapper for
the fur traders. He signed an
adhesion to Treaty No. Six in 1876 as
chief of his band, and settled on the
Michel Reserve north-west of Edmonton at Rivière Qui Barre. He
died in 1910" ("Overlanders in
Alberta," p. 2n). Dobson Prest wrote
that the "man that guided us here is
the Co. mail carrier" (to "Mamma
from Edmonton," 22 July 1862).
Alexander Fortune wrote that the
Overlanders found Michel "true,
faithful, efficient and agreeable, and
most useful" ("Collection," p. 35)
and that later at Edmonton Michel
went to the trouble of collecting
"some Indians and other half-breeds
and serenaded our company two
nights by singing and drum beating
and dancing Indian style and showing us the exciting war dance" (ibid.,
p. 38).

48. A comparison of John Sellar's and
Alexander Fortune's accounts of one
particular bridge-building episode is
most amusing. Here is Fortune's
version:

> On a certain Saturday night we
> reached a point of difficulty
> [near a swollen stream]....
> Many of our party were uneasy
> [because of the threat of Indian
> attack and the danger of flood].
> ...These men proposed to
> work on the following Sabbath;
> by building a bridge.... Those
> of us who objected to work or

travel on Sunday were in the
minority on this occasion. The
large majority was at the bridge
and they worked hard and
anxiously until they finished.
...Several deputations from
the new camp visited us and
advised us to come over for fear
the flood might rise and carry it
away. We told them kindly we
would trust the God of the
Sabbath, who also ruled the
floods. Our sleep was sweet and
our witnessing for God was well
rewarded. No floods increased;
we crossed the bridge Monday
morning. The bridge builders
did not show a spirit of
animosity towards our benefit-
ting by their hard work (ibid., p.
36).

Sellar, however, did show some
animosity, at least in his diary, where
he wrote that "those who thought
themselves above Sabath breaking,
(Like the person who puts himself on
a par with the thief by receiving the
stollen goods)...put themselves on
a par with the Sabath breakers as they
called us by pertaking of the benifits
of the bridge, & that as soon as they
could" ("Journal," p. 68).

49. "Edmonton, which is quite as large
as Fort Garry, is wholly built of
wood, and is furnished with strong
bastions and palisades; the latter,
however, being rather rotten....It
stands on a high steep bank immediately overhanging the river, about
100 feet above the water....the farm
attached to the establishment,
though the only one in the Saskatchewan, is of very small size, not
exceeding 30 acres. On a hill behind
the fort stands a windmill, in which
the stones were made by splitting a
granite boulder...and these, as may
be supposed, are not very serviceable,"
wrote Dr. Hector of the Palliser
group. He also noted that the boats
for the Saskatchewan river trade
were built at Edmonton and that
therefore there was a "larger staff of
tradesmen and servants there than at
any of the other posts of the district.
In all they have about 50 employés
here, and the usual population
within the fort is about 150 souls."

Hector mentioned the lack of good wood near the fort, which had to be brought from white spruce stands about fifteen kilometres away and commented on the seams of coal in the river banks, some of which had burned and transformed the clay into something like tile or brick (see Spry, *Palliser Papers*, pp. 201-2).

50. Clerks at all the HBC posts visited by the Overlanders kept daily journals, but as far as is known, only those from Edmonton and Kamloops have survived from the period. Some excerpts from the Fort Edmonton Journal provide additional information and some insight into how veterans of the country reacted to the travellers (see also introduction note 26 for excerpts describing the Symington and Redgrave parties at Edmonton):

Monday 21st [July]. Arival of the Canadian and Amarican miners. Rain part of the day a large party of miners apeered across the river...no one crossed this day men ware sent down for a boat bellow. Tuesday 22nd. Weather some better men arived with the boat J.E.B. [Joseph Edward Brazeau] acompanied by Mr. Alexander went across to convince the miners to pass by the Coutonais [Kootenay] pass, but found them obstinate and determined to go by Jaspers House. Wednesday 23rd. We had a shower or two this day half of the party crossed to day...freemen crowded inn to trade with miners. Thursday 24th. Weather better at least no rain Called to one of thair assemblies some of the miners undesided by what pass to go, after our representation of the nealy imposibility of getting through. Friday 25th. Weather unseteled men doing verry little on account of the miner the magority we understand if not all have desided to go by Jaspers House Pass. Saturday 26th. Weather as yesterday Cpts. McMicman Watty and Robertson made arangement with Andrew Cardinal to

take them as far as tete Jones Cash men doing nothing but trading with the miners. Sunday 27th. Revd Mr. Woolsey held forth in the fort in the morning and in the miners camp in the evening Capt Robertson went to St. Albert acompanied by J.E.B. on some baisness with the guide and returned in the evening. Monday 28th. Weather Stormy men doing verry little as we have no provisions miners making preparation slowly, thay have desided in taking the most of thair oxen with them. Tuesday 29th. Rain most part of the day Mineors making preparation still, James Ward returned from the plains with empty carts and starving after being out twenty nine days. Wednesday 30th. Cloudy no rain untill night Miners left for St. Albert with horses and oxen packed, several of the men caried besides thair Gun forty five or fifty pounds, on thair backs.

51. Joseph Edward Brazeau (?-1870) was born to a prominent Creole family in St. Louis, Missouri. He entered the American fur trade about 1830, serving at posts on the Yellowstone and Missouri Rivers, and then joined the HBC. He spoke English, French, and Spanish, as well as Saulteaux, Stony, Sioux, Cree, Blackfoot, and Crow. In 1850 he took charge of Jasper House, and later served at Rocky Mountain House and at Edmonton. His wife was Marguerite Brabant, and they had eight children. Captain Palliser spoke of Brazeau with great friendliness and with respect for his competence. Brazeau died at St. Albert (see MacGregor, *Overland by the Yellowhead*, p. 71; Spry, *Palliser Papers*, pp. 385, 592; Dempsey, "Overlanders in Alberta," p. 3n. Further biographical information about Brazeau has been kindly supplied by A.D. Ridge, archivist, and the heritage historian at the Archives of Alberta (to present editor, 4 April 1978).

For biographical note on William Christie, see text note 14.

52. The person in question was probably the well-known plainsman, Peter Erasmus, who worked for Woolsey for two different periods before 1862, totalling about three years. Erasmus was a successful gold miner, having visited the Pend d'Oreille mines in British Columbia about 1859, where he amassed quite a sum of money. According to his own statement, Erasmus made a trip to Fort Garry shortly after leaving Woolsey's employ for the second time early in 1862, so it is entirely possible that he met the Overlanders briefly at Portage la Prairie, although in dictating his memoirs more than sixty-eight years later it is understandable that he had forgotten the incident (see *Buffalo Days and Nights*, pp. 155-59, passim).

The Reverend Thomas Woolsey (1818-94) was born in Lincolnshire. He served in the Methodist Church there before coming to Canada in the early 1850's. He was ordained in 1855 at London, Ontario, and immediately posted to Edmonton. Soon after his arrival he reopened the Pigeon Lake mission. For the next five years he ranged over the entire upper North Saskatchewan. In 1860 he established a mission at Smoky Lake. In 1863 this was moved south to the North Saskatchewan River and named Victoria (now Pakan). The following year he left the Edmonton district and went to England for a visit. He returned to Canada and served at Farnham, Quebec, and various Ontario points retiring in 1885. He died in Toronto (A.D. Ridge to the present editor, 4 April 1978).

For an account of Woolsey's mission work in Alberta and personal glimpses of the endearing old gentleman, see Erasmus, *Buffalo Days and Nights*.

The Overlander Dobson Prest wrote of Woolsey to his mother from Edmonton, 22 July 1862:

I have had a long chat with Mr. Wolsey he is now taking his dinner in no. 2 tent. He is an Englishman, unmarried, is much such a man in manner as well as appearance as Mr. Cobb. He says he cannot get flour here half the time, says he has met in with droves of stone Indians that would try to kill him in two ways, one with eating, the other with kissing. They would kiss him and he would have to eat in every tent. He has eaten skunks and many other delicacies that I have not tasted, has been in this country 7 years.

53. The names of most of the Overlanders who stopped at Edmonton are not known. However, James Kelso and John Malcolm were two of them (see text note 41 above) and Erastus Hall a third. The three were all of the Acton party, and A.L. Fortune describes how they were out hunting one day east of the mountains, "when Erastus Hall accidentally shot himself by hauling a gun out of his cart with muzzel in hand" ("Collection," p. 41). The Glassford brothers, of Ottawa, also stayed in Edmonton, but by March, 1863, they had made their way through "the Kootanie pass" to Walla Walla, Washington. "It appears that quite a number of Canadians who came overland last year have taken their way to Washington Territory" ("Men Left Behind on the Fraser," *Colonist*, 4 March 1863).

54. Thomas Clover (1809-?) "was one of the 'Forty-Niners' who went to California, and by 1858 he was on the Fraser River. In the 1860's he drifted into the Edmonton area with Timolean Love and was washing gold on the North Saskatchewan at what came to be called 'Clover's Bar' (now Clover Bar). He later left the North Saskatchewan and when last heard of in 1897 was at Leroy, North Dakota" (A.D. Ridge to present editor, April 1978). See also introduction note 26 on Timolean Love.

55. The highest elevation of Boundary Pass is 2,164 metres, and of North Kootenay Pass 2,028 metres, compared with Yellowhead which is 1,121 metres. The former passes lie about 966 kilometres south of Yellowhead Pass. As noted in intro-

duction note 1, Sinclair Pass (1,421 metres) does not lie in the Rockies. It is possible that by Sinclair Pass the HBC men meant one of the two actually used by Sinclair to cross the Rockies, White Man (2,075 metres) or Kananaskis (2,378 metres). According to Spry, " 'Kootonais Pass' was a familiar term, though it is nowhere clear exactly what it meant.... Scarcely anyone at the time of the Palliser expedition had dependable knowledge" of southern mountain pass routes (*Palliser Papers*, p. lxix).

The Leather Pass acquired its name because in the days of the fur trade there was always a shortage of big game—and consequently of leather—in New Caledonia. The HBC decided in 1825 that shipments of leather goods, which had up to that time been sent into what is now northern B.C. via the Peace River route, were now to be forwarded via Fort Assiniboine and picked up from the Jasper area by men coming up the Fraser River from Fort George. However, the difficulties of the new route were so great that after only about four years, the company began sending leather through Dunvegan and the Peace River route again (see MacGregor, *Yellowhead*, pp. 42-43, 52, 54, 71).

56. Catholic Church records kindly provided by Father Dr. E.O. Drouin, O.M.I., Oblate archivist, of Edmonton, show that André Cardinal was born in 1829, son of Jacques Cardinal and Marguerite or Marianne Desjarlais, a Metis. André was married to Rosalie Berland or Breland, daughter of F. and T. Karakouti—"of the Iroquois tribe near Jasper House and now of Grand Cache"—and they had two children, Julie and Justine, by 1862. He was employed by the HBC at different times and was in charge of Jasper House in 1855-56. In 1858 Cardinal guided Henry John Moberly from Edmonton to Jasper, where the latter remained in charge for four years. In his old age, Moberly claimed to have been the first white man to mark the trail and take a pack train over it; but it seems likely that honour should fall to J.E. Brazeau, whose "lobsticks" and cache along

the way were pointed out to Dr. James Hector by his guides in 1859 (see text note 51 above and Mac-Gregor, *Yellowhead*, p. 71).

In 1859 Cardinal accompanied the Earl of Southesk from Lac Ste Anne to Jasper (Southesk, *Saskatchewan and the Rocky Mountains*, pp. 169, 172, 175). In May of 1863 André told Milton and Cheadle all he knew about the Yellowhead route and the fate of the "emigrants," or "Yankees," as Cheadle called the Overlanders, adding that near the place where Cardinal had turned back, after guiding them as far as he could, the Thompson River travellers had "like the Israelites of old, viewed the promised land, the hills of Cariboo being visible in the far distance ... but he was uncertain whether the emigrants intended to reach Cariboo direct, or steer for Fort Kamloops" (see Milton and Cheadle, *North-West Passage by Land*, p. 193, and also Cheadle, *Journal*, p. 145).

André was thus one of the pioneers of the Lac Ste Anne to Jasper route, which is now closely followed by the modern Yellowhead highway. The Cardinal family was well-known throughout the prairies in fur-trading days. André's father, Jacques, was one of seventeen children of Joseph Cardinal (1756-1856), who was from St. Laurent near Montreal, and his wife Louise Frobisher, a Metis. Joseph, "a most loquacious person," had been a companion to Sir Alexander Mackenzie in 1787 and to David Thompson in 1799 and served as a guide and interpreter with the North West Company and the HBC in the Edmonton-Peace River-Rocky Mountain area. This patriarch took three wives during his long life, but he does not appear to have been the only progenitor of Cardinals in the west, for the number of descendants still living there is vast indeed. In fact, a number of Alberta place names derive from Cardinals. For more details see sources cited. (Other information comes from A.D. Ridge to present editor, 4 April 1978; Lynn Huhtala to present editor, 16 May 1978.)

A "freeman," as TM uses the

word, was the term applied to "a former employee of a fur company who elected to remain in the interior as a free hunter, or sometimes, as a free trader" (*Dictionary of Canadianisms*).

57. The correct French name for Tête Jaune Cache has been substituted for McMicking's original "Tête-jeune-cache." The place was named for Pierre Hatsinaton, an Iroquois who apparently had a liberal admixture of European blood which gave him his light hair. (Several hundred Iroquois Indians from the east emigrated to the far western plains about 1800. They were much hated by the Indians native to that area, but they were valued by the white fur traders for their daring and knowledge of their adopted territory.) Tête Jaune was hired in 1820 by the HBC. The Cache was named "Tête Jaune's"—there are many spelling variants—in company records by 1826. In 1828 John Tod, factor at Kamloops, reported that Tête Jaune and his family had been killed in New Caledonia by their enemies, the Beaver Indians. For more information see MacGregor, *Yellowhead*, pp. 1-3, 26-28, 50-51, passim.

58. The mission of St. Albert at Big Lake was established by Father Lacombe in 1861 and named by Bishop Taché for Lacombe's patron. It was meant to minister to the Blackfeet, as it was nearer Edmonton, where they often gathered, than was the mission at Lac Ste Anne which ministered mainly to Crees. However, the settlers around St. Albert were mostly Métis, or, as John Sellar put it, "half-breeds from Caughnawaga" ("Journal," p. 72). It is true that at least some of the St. Albert Métis had Iroquois blood in their veins, being descended in part from those eastern hunters and guides who had drifted west with the fur trade in the late eighteenth century.

Milton and Cheadle described St. Albert ("St. Albans," as they called it) in 1863 as a collection of twenty houses built on the rising ground near the lake and river, which was spanned by a sturdy bridge. The mission consisted of a small white house for the priest, a chapel, school, and, in 1863, a residence for the nuns. The Overlanders did not meet Father Lacombe (see introduction note 24). The priest in charge was Father René Rémas.

59. Lac Ste Anne was the first permanent Roman Catholic mission for Crees and Métis established on the upper Saskatchewan. It was also the site of the first church built west of Red River. The mission was ordered built by Jean-Baptiste Thibault, who moved into it with Joseph Bourassa, also an Oblate priest, in 1844. Father Lacombe made his headquarters there from 1852 to 1861.

In 1862 there were three "Grey Nuns" stationed at the mission: Zoë Leblanc (Sister Emery), aged 35, Sister Adèle Lamy, 27, and Marie Jacques (Sister Alphonse), 26. These Catholic sisters conducted a small school and managed a dispensary. They were, according to James Schubert, the only white women seen by his mother Catherine on her journey with the Overlanders. The sisters nursed TM's companion William Morrow back to health after he was injured by his ox for the second time on the trek (see text note 22, above).

The superiority of the Big Lake area as a farming district induced many of the Lac Ste Anne settlers to move to the new mission of St. Albert in 1862, as the Overlanders' guide André Cardinal had done and as the three Grey Nuns did in 1863. For full historical details, see E.O. Drouin, *Lac Ste-Anne Sakahigan* (Edmonton: Editions de l'Hermitage, 1973).

60. Colin Fraser (ca. 1805-67) was in charge of this post, which he had opened only a few months before. Fraser, born in Scotland, came to North America in 1827 as Sir George Simpson's private piper, and accompanied the famous HBC governor on his tours of inspection throughout the Northwest. According to Milton and Cheadle, Fraser had been thirty-seven years in the country without a break by 1863. He had spent seventeen of those years at Jasper House; had not been to Fort Garry in thirty-five years; had not been east of

Edmonton in fifteen; yet he was "as happy and contented as possible" (*North-West Passage by Land*, p. 200). He and his native wife had a large family, twelve at this time, mostly grown-up daughters according to A.L. Fortune. Fraser's only regret was the "want of civilized opportunities for [his] dear family in the wilderness" ("Collection," p. 43). According to James Schubert, Fraser "played [the Overlanders] off with bagpipes" ("Reminiscences," p. 6. See also MacGregor, *Yellowhead*, p. 81; Eric J. Holmgren and Patricia Holmgren, *Over 2000 Place Names of Alberta*, 3d ed. [Saskatoon: Western Producer, 1976], p. 61).

61. William Phillips recorded the departure of McMicking's company from the mission with this ominous anecdote: "Our trip thus far was a continuous delight, but our good time had ended. It was fairly pleasant to St Ann's settlement, but, leaving this place in the morning I heard an Indian laugh, and exclaim in French, "they are on the road to H[el]l!" ("Reminiscences," pp. 7-8).

62. The Lake of Many Hills is now known as Lake Isle. It was noted as "Isle Lake" on Palliser's map. John Sellar calls it 'Hilly, (or Island) Lake" ("Journal," p. 76). All the names reflect the fact that there are numerous islands in the lake, which is about 5 kilometres long.

63. The smoke was not coming from a volcano, but from a large fire in the coal bed, "a small burning mountain" according to A.L. Fortune. The Redgrave party's guide stated that it had been burning "for generations": "sometimes it is all Fire—& then for years only Smoke" (Redgrave, "Papers," p. 275). Fires in the coal beds in the Elk River, Smoky River, and other parts of what is now Alberta were frequently mentioned by early travellers (see Dempsey, "Overlanders in Alberta," p. 6n.; MacGregor, *Yellowhead*, p. 22).

64. Lobstick River, named after J.E. Brazeau's "lobsticks" or limbed standing trees marking the trail (see MacGregor, *Yellowhead*, p. 71; also text note 56 above), flows from Chip Lake, originally known as Buffalo

Chip or Buffalo Dung Lake (see Dempsey, "Overlanders in Alberta," p. 7n; Holmgren, *2000 Place Names of Alberta*, pp. 56, 164. For another description of this "horrible" road, see Dobson Prest to father, 14 December 1862.

65. The section described by TM lay somewhere in the Niton area of what is now Alberta according to J.G. MacGregor (*Yellowhead*, p. 81).

66. James Willox and William Gilbert (see text note 1, above) were among several men who, against André Cardinal's advice, tried to wade the river rather than ride across on their animals. They were towed to shore by men on horseback, and "were so far gone . . . they had to be carried out of the water" (Sellar, "Journal," p. 82). A.L. Fortune's story of the rescue has a more romantic flavour: "There was one of the St. Catherine men who stepped too far down stream into deep water, and was being carried away with the swift current, but our noble guide Andrew, was on hand and made his horse carry him after the drowning man, and saved him as only an expert could have done" ("Collection," p. 45).

67. Just before this point, Andre Cardinal, who apparently enjoyed entertaining and instructing his charges about the history of the trail, arranged to lead the Overlanders through "timber not so thick as to obstruct our progress but . . . sufficient to hide the mountains from view. When at the low flat we soon walked out of all timber and there not many hundred yards from us, it seemed, towered the Great Rocky Mountains. Rock from bottom to top and no slope for soil or trees. They gave us a surprise that the guide enjoyed. He wanted to see the effect of this sudden view" (Fortune, "Collection," p. 47).

68. Hugh Dempsey has identified Prairie River as Maskuta Creek ("Overlanders in Alberta," p. 8n). It is still sometimes known as Prairie Creek, also as Clearwater River. The name in Cree is *mas-kioo-te-oo* (Holmgren, *2000 Place Names of Alberta*, p. 224).

69. There is no mountain called Mount Lacomb or Lacombe in the Jasper

area. Dempsey has tentatively identified this mountain as Roche Ronde ("Overlanders in Alberta," p. 8n).

Roche Miette (2,316 metres) rises 1,220 metres above the valley floor. Mr. Rory Flanagan, superintendent of Jasper National Park, has suggested that TM's "stupendous pile of rocks" might refer to the "lower talus slopes of Roche Miette which are quite extensive" (to the present editor, 31 March 1978). Early travellers were just as impressed with the area as TM was. Paul Kane wrote of his visit on 2 November 1846 that "it is scarcely possible to conceive the intense force with which the wind howled through a gap formed by the perpendicular rock called 'Miette's Rock,' 1500 feet high, on the one side, and a lofty mountain on the other. The former derives its appellation from a French voyageur, who climbed its summit and sat smoking his pipe with his legs hanging over the fearful abyss" (quoted in MacGregor, *Yellowhead*, pp. 65-66). But it is MacGregor's opinion that this story of the naming of Roche Miette is a tall tale invented by Kane's companions and that the name is really a corruption of the Cree word for the mountain sheep of the region, *my-a-tick* (see ibid.). Irene Spry, taking the anecdote more seriously, comments that Miette was an HBC servant who lived in the vicinity of Jasper Lodge and who "besides hunting, was occupied in the 1830's hauling coal." She also mentions that in February, 1859, Dr. Hector tried to climb the mountain with Henry John Moberly, but had to give up when "the great cubical block which forms the top of the mountain, still towered above us for 2,000 feet" (*Palliser Papers*, pp. 374-75).

70. The trail here led over Disaster Point. When the water was low enough, travellers preferred to skirt the point in the river, but at other times they had to climb over it. Ross Cox of the North West Company was one of the first to describe the road, which he with a large brigade had to cross from west to east in 1817. He wrote that it was "extremely steep. The horses surmounted it with great labour; and the knees of the majority of our party were put to a severe test in the ascent" (MacGregor, *Yellowhead*, p. 21). On the day of the Overlanders' ascent André Cardinal called a meeting to decide whether to avoid Disaster Point trail by crossing to the other side of the river. But the route on the other side would have entailed fording some dangerous rivers, so, as "there was a great many bad swimmers in the company," it was decided to try the ascent. At the top, a horse belonging to H. Blachford (or "Blanchford") "canted end over end about 1400 feet down" but was rescued intact (Sellar, "Journal," p. 89-90).

71. The original Jasper House was built in 1813 at the north end of Brulé Lake by François Decoigne and Jasper Hawse of the North West Company and called Rocky Mountain or Rocky Mountain Portage House. Hawse remained in charge of it for several years. The new Jasper House, built in 1829 by Michel Klyne several kilometres farther up the valley at the lower end of Jasper Lake, near the mouth of the Snake Indian River, was finally closed in 1884.

At the time of the Overlanders' journey, Jasper House was not occupied, though it was still occasionally used for shelter by HBC men crossing the mountains and as a station for keeping company horses. J.E. Brazeau was in charge of its intermittent operation in 1862 (see MacGregor, *Yellowhead*, pp. 22, 24, 39).

72. The names Russian Jack, Black Mountain, and Smith's Peak are not known today, nor can they be found in old maps or gazetteers. Hugh Dempsey believes that "Russian Jack" and "Smith's Peak" are probably McMicking's "anglicizing of 'Roche Jacques' and 'Roche de Smet.'" Black Mountain has not been identified ("Overlanders in Alberta," p. 9n).

73. It is possible the Californians had joined TM's party at Edmonton. They may, like Timoleon Love's group of four in 1860, have crossed the mountains from British Colum-

bia, probably by one of the southern passes rather than the Yellowhead, for McMicking implies that no one in his group but the guide knew anything of the route to Tête Jaune Cache. However, at least a few Overlanders from Canada, including James Wattie and I.D. Putnam, had spent some time in California during the gold rush years there.

74. According to J.G. MacGregor, since the Overlanders were now on the west (what TM called the north) side of the river, this site was actually a heap of rotting logs that had once been "a shack built in 1825 by Joseph La Rocque on Cottonwood Creek just north of present day Jasper, and which La Rocque called Mountain House. George Simpson decided the same year that the post was unnecessary and it was abandoned but provided shelter for travellers for many years" (*Yellowhead*, p. 37).

Joseph (possibly Joseph-Félix) Larocque (c. 1787-1866) was a veteran of the fur trade. Probably born at L'Assomption, Quebec, he served with the XY Company and the North West Company before being accepted as a chief trader with the HBC. As a representative of the NWC he built a post at Kamloops just a few weeks after rival Alexander Ross of J.J. Astor's Pacific Fur Company established a foothold there in 1812 (see text note 96, below). After the amalgamation of the NWC with the HBC in 1821, Larocque served at Edmonton House and Lesser Slave Lake and in the English River district. For details of his career, see E.E. Rich, "Joseph Larocque," *DCB* 9:456-57.

The original Henry's House was built in the winter of 1810-11 by William Henry, a cousin of Alexander Henry the Younger and an associate of David Thompson. The camp must have been set up just after Thompson left William Henry in the Jasper valley with their party's horses on December 29 and "set out with dogs and sleds to make the final dash across the Rocky Mountains to the Columbia river" (Richard Glover, *David Thompson's Narrative 1784-1812* [Toronto: Champlain Society,

1962], p. 318). There is some doubt about the exact location of Henry's House. According to Elliott Coues, Thompson's readings put it "precisely" at the confluence of the Miette and Athabasca Rivers, apparently on the east bank of the Athabasca (*The Manuscript Journals of Alexander Henry and of David Thompson 1799-1814* [New York: Francis P. Harper, 1897], 2:642). J.G. MacGregor discusses the evidence for other locations, showing that Thompson gave three different readings for the latitude. One reading would put the camp at the same latitude as Jasper Park Lodge, one would place it to the north between Annette and Edith lakes, and the third would have it at a point north of Edith Lake. Dr. MacGregor concludes that Henry's House stood in sight of Lac Beauvert, not too far from Jasper Park Lodge, just below the mouth of the Miette. This site would be quite close to the latitude of Larocque's House, although on the opposite bank of the Athabasca (MacGregor, *Yellowhead*, p. 13). Henry's House was probably abandoned when the first Jasper House was built in 1813 according to V.G. Hopwood.

75. Cow-dung or Yellowhead Lake was also known as Buffalo Dung Lake (see Milton and Cheadle, *North-West Passage by Land*, p. 245).

76. Roasted skunk was a dish André Cardinal seems to have fancied. In August 1859 he shot a skunk near the McLeod River and offered some to the Earl of Southesk, who "saw it roasting whole over the Iroquois' fire, looking awfully hideous, robbed of its skin and ears, and shorn of the bushy tail which in life had added something to its beauty." Next day, Southesk reported, "as a matter of curiosity I had a hind leg of the skunk for breakfast. It tasted like suckling-pig; very white, soft, and fat, but there was a suspicion of *skunkiness* about it that prevented me from finishing the plateful" (*Saskatchewan and the Rocky Mountains*, p. 175).

77. That is, William, not Alexander, Fortune (see introduction note 53).

According to DeWitt's "Arrival of

a Party of Overland Immigrants,"
Colonist, 3 November 1862, there
were thirty-six Thompson River
travellers. DeWitt, whose first name
is unknown, was one of them.

78. The discipline which characterized
the Queenston party was evident to
the end. At the Cache on 1 September, R.B. McMicking wrote: "Four of
our men conclude to go overland the
rest of the way to Cariboo with the
animals we therefore thought it
proper to disband the company at
this Point & therefore had a meeting
to that effect this morning and we
started on the raft at 2:40 P.M. & left
the others preparing for a start this
evening" ("Journal," p. 29).

79. The other St. Thomas men who went
off on this side-trip were R.P. Mead,
who settled at New Westminster as a
painter and decorator for a short time
starting in December, 1862 (Schubert, "Reminiscences," p. 11); Frank
Penwarden, who, as TM later mentions, was drowned in the Thompson
River near Kamloops; and Mr.
DeWitt, who supplied the *Colonist*
with an account of the trials of the
Thompson River travellers (see text
note 77, above).

80. Apparently the rapids were located in
what is called the Grand Canyon of
the Fraser, west of Toneka Lake
between the railway points of Long-
worth and Sinclair Mills, about one
hundred and sixty kilometres from
Fort George as the crow flies and a
little more than that from Tête Jaune
Cache. Some observers have called
this canyon more fearsome than the
famous Hell's Gate on the Lower
Fraser. The actual distance covered
by the Overlanders on the river to this
point was of course much greater, for
as John Sellar pointed out, "the river
wound back and forth across the
Valley so that it more than doubled
the distance shown by any Map"
("Journal," p. 100; see also text note
98, below, on distances).

81. Originally in Redgrave's party,
Carroll joined McMicking at Fort
Garry. It is not clear who rescued
McKenzie and Carroll. Wade says it
was the men on the Queenston raft,
but there is no mention of the
incident in R.B. McMicking's diary.

William McKenzie, of Whitby,
eventually settled at Kamloops and at
one time worked for the Hudson's
Bay Company there (Fortune, "Collection," p. 53). Eustace Pattison
(1843-62) was a shy and quiet young
man, "a keen student of biology"
who was "born at Launceston,
Cornwall, England, son of Samuel
Rowles Pattison, a London solici-
tor" (Wade, *Overlanders,* p. 119). He
was one of the Britishers attracted to
the overland route by the misleading
advertisements of the British Overland Transit Company. Arriving in
Toronto and finding that there was
no proper provision for further travel
with the said company, he joined the
Toronto party and later McMicking's group at Fort Garry.

82. For a biographical note on Robertson, see text note 22. Robert Warren
(1832-89) was born in Kingussie,
Scotland. In 1862 he was a farmer at
Acton. According to John Sellar, he
was a cousin to A.C. Robertson. The
rescue of Warren and Douglas was
carried out by A.L. Fortune and
William Sellar, who with the canoe
carried on their raft (a safety
precaution all the large rafts observed) took the men off the island
(see Fortune, "Collection," pp. 54-
55; Sellar, "Journal," p. 102). Sellar's
narrative indicates that this mishap
occurred a distance upriver from the
Grand Canyon, on 14 September.
Even before reaching the Grand
Canyon, the Lower Canadians in the
party found the rapids in the Fraser
worse than anything in their home
province, and there was "no comparison between [the rapids on the Niagara between] the Falls and Queenston, the worst spot in it does not compare with these" (Dobson Prest to
father, 15 December 1862).

83. For a detailed account of the
drowning of John Carpenter, who
was Alexander's friend and companion, see Alexander, *Diary and
Narrative,* pp. 23-25. The *British
Columbian,* 25 October 1862, reported the drowning deaths not only
of "James Carpenter, a Barrister from
Toronto," but also of Alexander and
his companions H. Fletcher, from
Montreal, Alfred Hancock, of Toron-

to, and David Jones from England, all of the Redgrave party. On 15 November, after a visit to the office of the paper from Fletcher, the editor contradicted the earlier report, except for the death of Carpenter. On 7 November, Alexander read of his supposed death while travelling via the Lillooet-Pemberton-Harrison Lake route to New Westminster.

Nothing more is known of the circumstances of Leader's death, except that he was of the Redgrave party, and had started earlier than Alexander, Carpenter, and friends from Tête Jaune Cache.

84. The fort was built by Simon Fraser near the junction of the Fraser and Nechako Rivers in 1807, the year before Fraser's trip down the river named for him to the Pacific Ocean. McMicking has confused the Stuart River which flows into the Nechako some distance northwest of Prince George with the Nechako itself. This is a common error of early maps.

Taken over in 1821 by the HBC and closed in 1823, the fort was re-opened in 1829 and continued in operation until 1915. Its site lay immediately to the south of the present city of Prince George, at what is called South Fort George. For more information see F.E. Runnalls, *A History of Prince George* (Vancouver, 1946).

85. Eustace Pattison was buried in a small canoe, "split and shaped into a coffin" (Fortune, "Collection," pp. 59-60).

86. Shortages of food at Fort George were not uncommon. Even on the game-rich prairies, HBC posts were often short of provisions for their own people by 1862 (see, for example, the Fort Edmonton Journal entry for Tuesday, 29 July 1862, quoted in text note 50, above). The Rennie brothers (see introduction note 27, above) also reported that shortly after their arrival at Edmonton on 27 August 1862, Governor Dallas visited the fort on a tour of Rupert's Land. "He was received with a salute of cannon, but the utmost difficulty was found in entertaining him properly, as the Fort was out of provisions; some were, however, obtained from Pere

Le Compte [Lacombe], the Catholic missionary there, who had just returned from Red River" ("A Melancholy Diary," *Colonist*, 11 July 1863). The Rennie brothers gave evidence of severe shortages at Fort George in the winter of 1862-63.

87. Thomas Charles (1824-85) was born at Split Lake, Rupert's Land, son of HBC factor John Charles. Richard Alexander noted in his diary that "Mr. Charles, the Factor, studied under my old master, Trotter, when he had a boarding school at Mussel-burgh [near Edinburgh]. Charles has a brother in charge of Fort Hope, further down the river" (*Diary and Narrative*, p. 27). The brother was William Charles, who served the HBC at Hope, Yale, Kamloops, and Victoria, and was eventually pro-moted to chief factor. Thomas appears to have spent nearly all his years with the company at different posts in the interior of northern B.C. Father Adrian Morice comments in a brief note that "William Todd, a young man without experience was first appointed to the new post [on a lake called Lhuz'Koez or Tluzkluz] (September, 1844), to be almost immediately replaced by a new-comer, Thomas Charles, who proved to be as careful and thrifty as the other was careless and negligent" (*Northern Interior*, p. 244). For the notice of death and obituary of Thomas Charles, see *Colonist*, 7 April 1862.

88. A.L. Fortune described meeting some Chinese goldwashers above Quesnel:

On landing we gave them a surprise; but settled their doubts by showing that we were travelling to Cariboo. Mr. Wattie questioned them; how much gold you catch here one day one man? One day one dollar someday four bittee, six bittee, one day long time, two dollars. How far Quesnelle River? Maybe twenty miles. Some six of them surrounded a dish of rice and bacon soup. Soup that they shovelled into their mouths with chopsticks instead of spoons. We had never seen specimens of that wonderful people before this time, except Mr. Wattie, who had been in California some years previous. They were wonderful to us, with their chopsticks, pigtail and sallow skin. They were smaller than our men ("Collection," pp. 62-63).

89. The Quesnel River was named after Jules Maurice Quesnel, an associate of Simon Fraser in 1808. Robert McMicking described the settlement at Quesnel as follows: "There is lots of Provision being two stores & eating Houses & other little buildings Indian Huts &c Meals 1.50 Each at Whitehall store flour 50 Dollars Salt 1 Dollar a pound Rice 55 cents Bacon 75 to 1.00 Beans 75 tea 2.00 per pound the day was very fine and pleasant I got my supper of a table for the first time in four months at Whitehall store" ("Journal," p. 31). For more information on Quesnel, see Gordon R. Elliott, *Barkerville, Quesnel, and the Cariboo Gold Rush.*

90. But the Overlanders' joy on reaching Quesnel did not last long. John Sellar quickly sized up the depressing situation:

> The miners were just beginning to leave the mines on account of snow & many, in fact most of [them] for want of means to get provisions to exist on while prospecting their clames. An odd one now & then had done well, but not one out of every 500 who had gone there this season, As most of us were pretty well played out of money we concluded to sell our animals, picks shovells, & what clothing we did not wish to pack on our backs & rase enough take us to some other country where we could afford to live as no person at Carriboo could pretend to live, they mearly stayed & starved" ("Journal," pp. 108-9).

In March, 1863, A.L. Fortune, who had tramped in to Williams Creek the previous fall, sent a long letter assessing the practical problems of mining in Cariboo to the *Montreal Witness* (reprinted in the *Sarnia Observer*, 8 May 1863), which published it as a warning to Easterners contemplating emigrating to B.C. Fortune denounced the "hard-speculators, traders, packers, steamboat proprietors, house-letters, tavern-keepers, and editors, for holding out false inducements regarding the country" and stated that a man must have a minimum of $1,500 before he might even think of developing a claim in Cariboo.

91. The Thompson River travellers' route led up the McLennan River valley to Cranberry Lake (near today's Valemount), across the Canoe River, up the Camp River to Albreda Pass, and down the Albreda River to the point where it joins the North Thompson.

Cardinal took his thirty-two charges as far as the junction of the Albreda and North Thompson Rivers. Here, they made an attempt to cut a trail up the Thompson in a northwesterly direction, heading directly for Cariboo, but abandoned the effort after going about a mile. It was probably from this point that, as Cardinal told Milton and Cheadle, he and the Overlanders had seen the hills of Cariboo in the distance (see text note 56, above). Cardinal turned back to Edmonton; someone recorded the date and place of his departure, and the tree blazed for the purpose was found the next year by Milton and Cheadle and again nearly ten years later by members of the Canadian Geological Survey (see Wade, *Overlanders*, p. 111; Milton and Cheadle, *North-West Passage by Land*, p. 271). About 14 September the four St. Thomas men (see text note 79, above) met Cardinal on his way back at Albreda Lake.

92. The Overlanders named the spot where they abandoned the horses and stopped to build rafts "Slaughter Camp" because they also killed their oxen and dried the meat there. When the St. Thomas men caught up to them at this place on 18 September, they were still engaged in these activities. The next year Milton and Cheadle found "pack-saddles and harness, and great cedars cut down on every side, with heaps of chips and

splinters" at this spot, as well as the blazed tree with the name of the camp still clear. The location of "Slaughter Camp," which was probably not at the confluence of the North Thompson and the Albreda as TM suggests, is discussed in Appendix 2, "A Note on the Trail."

93. The long rapid was later named Murchison Rapids, but that name no longer appears on maps. However, the "Porte d'Enfer," a terrible canyon at the southern end of these rapids, can still be found. DeWitt, whose story of the trip appeared in the *Colonist* and was picked up by the *Toronto Globe*, asserted that the rough water continued for "fifteen miles" (see *Colonist*, 3 November 1862; "News from British Columbia," *Globe*, 9 December 1862).

94. For what little is known of William Strachan, see text note 41, above. Four men were involved in the accident which cost Strachan his life: the others were Archibald Thompson, John Fannin, and (possibly) William Fortune. They were in charge of a raft loaded with seven horses and one ox. It ran into Murchison Rapids, when Strachan and Fortune jumped off and tried to hold it, but it was swept away, smashing into a rock a short distance below and throwing Thompson and Fannin into the water. They managed to reach a rock in the stream and were stranded there when Strachan attempted to swim out to them with a line, but he was carried downstream and drowned. The two on the rock were rescued by Andrew Hales, assisted by Daniel McAlpine (see Wade, *Overlanders*, p. 112; Schubert, "Reminiscences, p. 9).

95. Possibly the reference is to Mad Rapids, a name suggested by Mary Balf, curator of the Kamloops museum (to the present editor, 6 June 1978). The mouth of the Mad River lies about 19 kilometres above present day Vavenby and about 41 kilometres south of the Porte d'Enfer canyon, which would put the rapids (that, according to Mary Balf, extend some distance from the mouth of the river and are shown as "Falls" and a small obstruction on modern maps),

in the approximate location described by TM. These rapids, DeWitt noted in the *Colonist*, 3 November 1862, were "about thirty miles long."

96. Milton and Cheadle describe the fort as follows:

> The Hudson's Bay Company's Fort at Kamloops is situated on the south bank of the Thompson, a few hundred yards below the junction of the northern with the southern branch. Opposite the fort the two streams flow distinct in a common channel, the turbid, glacier-fed river from the north contrasting with the limpid waters of the other, like the Missouri after its junction with the Mississippi. . . . Seven miles below, the river expands into Lake Kamloops, and issues from thence again clear and pellucid, to be lost at Lytton in the muddy and turbulent Fraser.
>
> The country round Kamloops is of the Californian character before described. Rolling hills, covered with bunch-grass and scattered pines, rise in every direction. The pasturage is very rich and extensive, and large bands of horses, herds of cattle, and flocks of sheep, are kept here by the Hudson's Bay Company (*North-West Passage by Land*, pp. 319-20).

In 1812 Alexander Ross had built a small post here for the American Pacific Fur Company, on the south side of the river junction. The same year Joseph Larocque of the NWC also built a small post at "Cum Cloups," northeast of the junction. In 1813 the American company sold out to its rival, and Larocque enlarged his post, which was left in charge of Ross for several years. In 1821, when the HBC and the NWC were joined, the fort continued as Thompson's River Post. In 1842 it was rebuilt on a site to the northwest of the river junction, with a 4.5-metre palisade, and seven buildings inside. In 1862 a new post, which was nearing completion when the Overlanders arrived, was built on the south side of the river. No fortification was included, as it was now seen to be unnecessary. A large garden and farm were established; there were also dwellings, storehouses, stables, and barns. A number of the Overlanders, including William Fortune and Augustus Schubert, went to work for the company here. They were in demand as workers in 1862, for smallpox and the mining excitement had decimated the ranks of labourers in the district (see Balf, *Kamloops*, pp. 6-14, 18-19).

The agent in charge of Kamloops in 1862 was Joseph William Mackay (1829-1900), or McKay, as he was known in HBC records, who was born at Rupert House on the west coast of Hudson's Bay, son of an HBC clerk. He was educated at Red River and entered the company service as a very young man, starting at Fort Vancouver on the Columbia in 1844 and ultimately rising to the rank of chief trader. In 1849-50 while at Victoria he obtained company permission to investigate the claim of an Indian from Winterhuysen Inlet that there was much coal near his home. In 1853 Mackay established a fort and coal mines at the site, called Nanaimo. From 1856 to 1859 Mackay was one of the first six members of the legislative assembly of the colony of Vancouver Island. Later he was in charge of the HBC posts at Yale and at Kamloops (1860-65), and then he was transferred again to Victoria where he was appointed chief factor. While in the HBC service he conducted a number of exploring expeditions, one from Kamloops to Tête Jaune Cache and overland to Williams Creek (the journey the Thompson River Overlanders were not able to make), looking for a practical telegraph route. Mackay married Helen Holmes in 1860, and they had four daughters and one son. He retired from the company in 1879 and after that became Indian agent at Kamloops. For more information, see Mackay's obituary, "A Pioneer of Pioneers," *Colonist*, 25 December 1900; Balf, *Kamloops*, pp. 13-14, 80-81; Vertical File, PABC.

Actually the Overlanders straggled in to Kamloops over a period of about two weeks, and some at least finished the journey by raft rather than on foot. The following laconic excerpts from the "Fort Kamloops Journal" record some sketchy details: Saturday 11th [October] Weather hazy all day—men at the fencing—also some transporting bricks—A Party of men have come down north River by Raft they are from Canada and the States and have come via Red River, Siskatchewan and Jasper House to Tete Jeaunes Cache thence to the Source of North River and down to this Point. . . . Monday 13th. . . . Employed Five Canadians to dig up Potatoes as well as Dusseau Boucho and Machie they took up only 121 Bushels and report the Crop as poor Indeed. . . . Tuesday 14. . . . Employed three more Canadians today. Wednesday 15th Another Party of some 15 more men arrived by the North Branch. Thursday 16th Employed two more men at $1.00 per day. Friday 17th A party [probably Augustus Schubert] has contracted to Build up one of the Old Houses taken over from here at the new place for $100.00. Tuesday 25th. Some Canadians arrived this evening with a large raft of dry weather [*sic*]. Sunday 26th. Another party is said to have arrived via the Tete Jeaunes Cache and North River.

97. The baby was apparently born on 14 October near the site of an Indian settlement which lay to the northeast of the river junction, near the old buildings of Larocque's post (see Balf, *Kamloops*, p. 19).

98. An attempt to calculate the actual distance by river between Tête Jaune Cache and Quesnel has been made using maps of a scale of 1:50,000. Even at this scale very large errors are possible, but these calculations indicate that McMicking's distances are over-estimated by as much as 25 per cent, except for the mileage from Fort

George to Quesnel, which appears low by about 10 to 15 per cent.

99. In almost all the Overlander journals and memoirs, the authors noted an improvement in health on the journey, particularly in resistance to infections and a growth in physical strength and endurance. Stephen Redgrave wrote, "I used to be a bad walker but I can travel my 25 miles a day now—altho I feel tired after it which makes me sleep sound a thing I hardly ever knew in Toronto" ("Papers," p. 215). Harkness informed his ·wife in a letter from Carlton House, 1 July 1862, "I have grown so tough . . . I have lost at least 20 pounds in flesh . . . but I am still perfectly healthy." Later, from Edmonton, 23 July, he wrote, "Indeed, I never was more healthy in my life" ("Letters"). John Nichols, the tuberculous patient Dr. Symington had persuaded to turn around and travel with the Overlanders from Breckenridge, Minnesota, (see introduction, note 23, above), was strong and well by the time he got to Edmonton, "with the ambition of a conqueror and much liked" (Fortune, "Collection," p. 43). A.L. Fortune himself had been "an invalid, more or less" during the ten years before the journey, but in 1862 he became healthy and remained so until old age. "Others spoke of their incapacity from various kinds of sickness. And long before we reached Edmonton we had no weak members in our party, none looking for medicines, doctors, nor nurses" (ibid., p. 38).

However, Dobson Prest noted at the end of 1863 that "nearly all the Overlanders [those, that is, that had remained in B.C.] were sick in Cariboo last season. . . . Physicians say that the hardships they suffered on the overland [trip] was the cause" (to brother from "Hurrican Hall," 25 December). In fact, there was much sickness among all the miners in Cariboo in 1863, no doubt because of unhealthy living conditions and poor nutrition (see Milton and Cheadle, *North-West Passage by Land*, p. 364; Cheadle, *Journal*, p. 252).

Selected Bibliography

HBCA   Hudson's Bay Company's Archives, Provincial Archives of Manitoba
PABC   Provincial Archives of British Columbia
SC/UBCL   Special Collections, University of British Columbia Library

Alexander, Richard Henry. *The Diary and Narrative of Richard Henry Alexander in a Journey across the Rocky Mountains.* Ed. with an Introduction by Neil Brearley. Richmond, B.C.: Alcuin Society, 1973.
———. "Diary of Richard Henry Alexander, April 29-December 31, 1862." Typescript copy, PABC.
Balf, Mary. *Kamloops: A History of the District up to 1914.* Kamloops: Kamloops Museum, n.d.
———. *The Overlanders and Other North Thompson Travellers.* Kamloops: Kamloops Museum, 1973.
Bancroft, Hubert Howe. *History of British Columbia.* San Francisco: History Company, 1890.
Begg, Alexander. *History of British Columbia from Its Earliest Discovery to the Present Time.* Toronto: William Briggs, 1894.
Caughey, John Walton. *The California Gold Rush.* Berkeley and Los Angeles: University of California Press, 1975.
Cheadle, Walter B. *Cheadle's Journal of Trip across Canada 1862-1863.* With Introduction and Notes by A.G. Doughty and Gustave Lanctot. Edmonton: Hurtig, 1971.
Dempsey, Hugh, ed. "The Overlanders in Alberta, 1862, by Thomas McMicking." *Alberta Historical Review* 4 (Summer 1966).
Dennis, Emma Louise McMicking. "Sketch of the Life of Thomas McMicking the Sixth." McMicking Family Papers in possession of Ronald McMicking, Victoria, B.C.
Elliott, Gordon R. *Barkerville, Quesnel, and the Cariboo Gold Rush.* Vancouver: Douglas and McIntyre, 1978.
Erasmus, Peter. *Buffalo Days and Nights, as told to Henry Thompson.* With an introduction by Irene Spry. Calgary: Glenbow-Alberta Institute, 1976.
Fort Edmonton Journal 1862. HBCA.
Fort Kamloops Journal December 16, 1860-November 30, 1862. PABC.
Fortune, Alexander Leslie. "Collection of Addresses and Narratives by A.L. Fortune." Typescript copy, SC/UBCL.
———. "The Overlanders of 1862." Ed. with an Introduction by G.D. Brown, Jr., *Kamloops Sentinel,* 27 November 1936, 1, 4, 8, 11, 15, 18, 22, and 24 December 1936.
Hargrave, Joseph James. *Red River.* Montreal: John Lovell, 1871.
Harkness, Robert. "Correspondence Outward: Personal Letters to his Wife, 1862-1865." Harkness Papers, PABC.
Harper, J. Russell. "William Hind and the Overlanders." *Beaver* (Winter 1971): 4-6, 7-15.
———. *William G.R. Hind 1833-1889.* Ottawa: National Gallery of Canada, 1976.
———. *William G.R. Hind 1833-1889: A Confederation Painter in Canada.* With an Introduction by Kenneth Saltmarche. Exhibition Catalogue. Windsor: Willistead Art Gallery, 1967.
Hind, Henry Youle. *Narrative of the Canadian Red River Exploring Expedition of 1857, and of the Assiniboine and Saskatchewan Exploring Expedition of 1858.* Reprint. Edmonton: Hurtig, 1971.

————. *A Sketch of an Overland Route to British Columbia*. Toronto: W.C. Chewett & Co., 1862.

Howard, J.K. *Strange Empire*. Toronto: Swan Publishing, 1965.

Hunniford, John. "Journal and Observations of John Hunniford, 1862. Overland to British Columbia from Ontario." SC/UBCL.

Kerr, J.B. *Biographical Dictionary of Well-Known British Columbians*. Vancouver: Kerr and Begg, 1890.

Macfie, Matthew. *Vancouver Island and British Columbia*. London: Longman, Green, Longman, Roberts, & Green, 1865. Facsimile ed., Toronto: Colés, 1972.

MacGregor, J.G. *Overland by the Yellowhead*. Saskatoon: Western Producer Book Service, 1974.

McMicking, James. "Sketch of the Life of Thomas McMicking (the Fourth)." McMicking Family Papers.

McMicking, Robert Burns. "Journal from Queenston, U.C., to British Columbia in 1862." Typescript copy, SC/UBCL.

————. "Thomas McMicking." Handwritten memoir, dated 3 December 1912, PABC.

McNaughton, Margaret. *Overland to Cariboo.* Toronto: William Briggs, 1896. Repr., with an Introduction by V.G. Hopwood, Vancouver: Douglas, 1973.

Milton, Viscount, and Cheadle, Walter B. *The North-West Passage by Land*. 7th ed. London: Cassell, Petter and Galpin, 1867.

Morice, A.G. *History of the Catholic Church in Western Canada from Lake Superior to the Pacific (1659-1895)*. 2 vols. Toronto: Musson, 1910.

————. *History of the Northern Interior of British Columbia 1660-1880*. London: John Lane, 1906.

Morton, Arthur Silver. *History of the Canadian West to 1870-71*. 2d. ed. Ed. Lewis G. Thomas. Toronto: University of Toronto Press, 1973.

Ormsby, Margaret A. *British Columbia: A History*. Toronto: Macmillan, 1958.

Prest, Dobson. "Correspondence Outwards, 1862 (and 1863)." Prest Papers, PABC.

Redgrave, Stephen. "Journals and Sundry Papers of Stephen Redgrave, 1852 to 1875." Typescript copy, PABC.

Rich, E.E. *History of the Hudson's Bay Company 1670-1870*. 2 vols. London: Hudson's Bay Record Society, 1958.

Russell, Ralph C. *The Carlton Trail: The Broad Highway into the Saskatchewan Country from the Red River Settlement 1840-1880*. Saskatoon: Prairie Books, 1971.

Schubert, James Armstrong. "Reminiscences: Notes of Conversation with James Armstrong Schubert, Retired Merchant, at Tulameen, 18 July 1930, recorded by R. Hartley." Typescript, PABC.

Sellar, John M. "Overland to Cariboo—Journal, April 22, 1862, to September 23, 1862." Typescript copy, SC/UBCL.

Southesk, Earl of. *Saskatchewan and the Rocky Mountains: A Diary and Narrative of Travel, Sport, and Adventure during a Journey through the Hudson's Bay Company's Territories in 1859 and 1860*. Edmonton: Hurtig, 1969.

Spry, Irene M., ed. *The Papers of the Palliser Expedition 1857-1860*. Toronto: Champlain Society, 1968.

Wade, Mark Sweeten. *The Overlanders of '62*. Archives Memoir no. 9. Victoria: King's Printer, 1931.

————. *The Cariboo Road*. Ed. Eleanor A. Eastick. Victoria: Haunted Bookshop, 1979.

Wallace, W. Stewart. *Macmillan Dictionary of Canadian Biography*. 3d ed. Toronto: Macmillan, 1963.

Index